'BRAVER

Peter Gurney was h
the Metropolitan Po
he retired in Decem   two children
and lives with his wife in south-east England.

Braver Men
Walk Away

═══

Peter Gurney

HarperCollins*Publishers*

HarperCollins*Publishers*
77–85 Fulham Palace Road,
Hammersmith, London W6 8JB

This paperback edition 1993
3 5 7 9 8 6 4 2

First published in Great Britain by
HarperCollins*Publishers* 1993

ISBN 0 00 637980 X

Set in Linotron Fournier by
Rowland Phototypesetting Ltd
Bury St Edmunds, Suffolk

Printed in Great Britain by
HarperCollinsManufacturing Glasgow

Contents

===

Acknowledgements

====

The author wishes to express his thanks to: Howard Reynolds, without whom this book would not have been written; my wife, Sheridan, who, despite my denials, insisted my life was of interest to others; Sir David Nicholas, Terry Spooner and the Press Association for their immeasurable assistance; Val Hudson and Karen Whitlock at Harper-Collins, and Don Short, who not only believed I had a book, but proved it.

For Sheridan – who waited.

It was the picture which did it: one moment it was hanging neatly on display in my office, the next it was on the floor. The morning of 7 February 1991 had been wholly unremarkable, the capital as grey and cold as the day I'd first joined the Explosives Office. But now, at 10.08, just as I was walking back to my desk in Cannon Row Police Station, cup of coffee in hand, everything changed. When a heavy bomb goes off in the distance you hear a rumble, the echo of the sound wave bouncing off buildings. When a bomb goes off near by you hear a distinct *crump!* like the one I'd just heard. It was followed by another lesser sound.

I sprinted to the doorway and yelled at the Control Room to find my driver.

Someone answered: 'You haven't been tasked yet.'

'When pictures start falling off my wall,' I shouted, 'I don't wait to be tasked.'

My Range Rover was in the yard, already loaded; my driver and I threw ourselves into it and hurtled out through the car park and into Whitehall. On my right I could see a vehicle on fire, a white Ford Transit van parked at an angle and away from the kerb. It was the only sign of anything wrong but it didn't explain the noise of the explosion – a sound like that and the Transit should have been blown to tiny pieces.

I grabbed an inspector who was trying to usher civilians away from the scene and asked him what had happened. 'That van,' he said. 'There's been an explosion in that van.'

This was obviously not going to get us very much further. I ran to the van. Through the flames and smoke I could see burning blankets hanging out of the back. I could also see something else: a hole in the roof and three mortar-launch tubes. I tried to get close enough to drag the blankets clear – they might have laundry marks on them (vital forensic evidence) – but the heat was too great and besides, I had heard only one major explosion. A mortar bomb contains 40 pounds of explosive; if two were still in the van then they could be cooked-off by the fire and blow up or be blasted anywhere along Whitehall. Because the mortars were being cooked-off rather than carefully aimed and launched, they could either travel the full distance of their 350-yard range or drop down anywhere along the flight path.

I went round to the front of the Transit and found the Inspector again; he was doing an outstanding job, marshalling his men to get people out of the way. I pointed to the area ahead of the blazing vehicle where a bomb might well fall. 'I want *that* area cleared,' I told him. 'I need a clear path two hundred yards wide and four hundred yards either end.'

At this point a TV camera crew turned up and caught me on film, waving my arms like a demented scarecrow in front of the blaze. It made for the kind of image television adores but right then I wasn't so much bothered about what TV was doing to me as what a couple of mortar bombs could do to Whitehall: 140 pounds of metal casing and explosive was likely to come crashing down through someone's roof from a height of over 250 feet. The buildings on either side of the flight path had to be cleared.

No sooner had I given these instructions than another police officer came running towards me from the direction of Downing

Street. Considering the circumstances, he was remarkably calm: 'There's been an explosion in the garden of Number Ten . . .'

I raced down Whitehall and turned into Downing Street. This was obviously the mortar bomb – the *crump!* I'd heard in my office. It was Brighton all over again; the terrorists were out to get the government itself, but this time it was a meeting of the War Cabinet, called into session to review the latest developments in the Gulf War.

The front door was open, a policeman standing just inside. I told him to warn everyone to stay inside and keep in the middle of the building. The officer then guided me through Number Ten's maze of corridors, down stairs and around corners and finally out into the rear garden. At the far end, the smoking remains of a cherry tree testified to how near the bombers had come to attaining their objective.

(There are many things which an explosives officer cannot know at the moment an incident is unfolding, and in this case I had no idea what sort of tree it was until much later – when I met Mrs Thatcher in a lift at New Scotland Yard. She had been visiting the Met's headquarters and I had been lunching with the Metropolitan Police Commissioner; when I was introduced to her as the Expo who had dealt with the Downing Street mortar attack she said: 'Oh, yes: that was when the poor cherry tree was destroyed.')

I walked across the wide expanse of lawn to the shallow crater near the tree. Judging by the crater's depth and the number of windows which had been smashed in the building it seemed that the mortar bomb had actually detonated above ground rather than on impact. It may, indeed, have actually hit the upper branches of the tree.

Just then another police officer materialized at my side and said something which both relieved and alarmed me: there *were* two more bombs, but they were lying outside on Treasury Green, a small grassed area next to Horse Guards Parade. According to the officer, it didn't look as though they had gone off . . . yet. He unlocked the gate for me and showed me the bombs. One was embedded tail first and had obviously malfunctioned; the explosive charge appeared to have ignited rather than detonated, vented out by a low-pressure explosion, and was now spread out all over the place. The other, however, lay on the ground, apparently intact.

I moved in close. They were big, these mortar bombs, 6½ inches in diameter and 4 feet long, with the fuze secured to the nose of the bomb by four large bolts. This type of fuze is very sensitive and, as the whole area had been cleared, I decided that now was the moment to remove it. Unfortunately I couldn't raise my driver on the radio because the buildings were blocking the signal, so the policeman raced to Number Ten's boiler room and collected an adjustable spanner which I needed to undo the bolts.

The fuze used in these bombs was quite a simple affair. In essence, it featured a heavy weight (the slider) which would be locked into place by a special safety pin. This pin would be ejected on firing the bomb and leave the weight free to move about inside the fuze body. On impact, the weight would strike the internal percussion cap and fire the bomb. It was therefore essential that the slider should not move now, otherwise there would be one Expo in the same state as the poor cherry tree.

Without moving the bomb, I examined as best I could the state of the fuze. Through the ¼-inch-diameter hole for the safety pin I could see the empty hole in the slider into which the pin had originally been set. To prevent the slider from moving, I needed some kind of safety pin of my own. I found a twig lying near by and wedged it into the hole. It wasn't ideal but I hoped it would hold long enough for me to deal with the fuze.

This was not going to be easy: I didn't dare risk any movement of the mortar because the twig might snap or fall out, leaving the weight free to slide about, yet I couldn't simply hold the mortar steady – it was far too big and heavy to manhandle. And thus it was that I came to be sitting astride a mortar bomb outside the garden at Number Ten, working away with the Prime Minister's spanner and trusting in the strength of a solitary twig.

It was cold out there on the bomb; I was thankful my fire-resistant trousers provided some degree of insulation against what I imagined to be the incisive chill of the mortar's casing. Snow was falling now, the flurries borne on a sharp-edged wind; all around, a frosting of white began to spread.

I concentrated on the bolts, bringing the spanner into position and ignoring the stabbing needles of cold upon my face. I was, after all, used to working in every kind of weather condition; being stuck out here with an unexploded bomb in a snowstorm was nothing to complain about. Indeed, in a disconnected kind of way I was thinking that the morning was quite pleasant, for despite the wind and the snow flurries a comfortable warmth was seeping through, a warmth that was getting hotter and hotter and –

They must have heard my anguished yell halfway across London. God Almighty! My balls were on fire.

Somehow I managed to get off the mortar without moving it and fell sideways. Finally I stood upright, or almost upright, wracked by the terrible burning pain and the realization that if I didn't do something about it soon I would never finish defuzing the damn bomb or sing anything other than soprano ever again.

I stared frantically around, looking for water – ice – anything to cool the blistering heat, and finally saw a small drift of snow against one of the trees. I opened my flies, scooped up the snow and thrust a handful into my trousers. If it meant frostbite, then so be it.

Bow-legged and sodden, I confronted the bomb again, thinking it was a bloody good job John Major and his Cabinet Ministers had been told to get into the centre of Number Ten, away from all the windows, otherwise they might have been looking out and wondering what the hell was going on. The bomb still lay there peacefully, giving no indication of its temperature. It couldn't possibly be that hot simply through firing; there had to be something else going on that I couldn't see. But second-guessing a bomb is something you never do; for all I cared it could start singing 'Rule Britannia!'. What mattered was that it was still there, still intact, and if I didn't get the fuze out soon . . .

There was no alternative: I sat down on it, clamped the spanner tight, wrenched it around a half-turn, then jumped up, waited for my backside to cool, sat down again, did another half-turn, jumped up again and waited again; sit down, half-turn, jump up, sit down, half-turn, jump up. I didn't dare look up at Number Ten to see if anyone was watching or if men in white coats were coming to take me away.

One bolt out, then another; sit down, half-turn, jump up. I had rarely met a more exhausting bomb in my life. Finally the work was finished. I eased the fuze out, stared inside the bomb and discovered that all the explosive had been burnt out. I could see a gap between the fuze housing and the bomb body, a gap caused either by internal pressure or structural distortion on impact. The burn-out had sent the casing almost incandescent, and I, all unwittingly, had chosen to sit astride it when it was almost at its hottest.

The area was now safe as well as secure and the clear-up could begin. I walked away with a preciseness of tread more appropriate to a ballet dancer than an explosives officer; I hoped no one would ask why.

The snow was falling much faster now, coming down from a low opaque sky to settle on the ground and gradually cover the gravel of Horse Guards Parade. It was the kind of surface you couldn't brush clear; if we were going to collect all the various bits of forensic evidence lying around – pieces of fuze, casing, explosive – then the search team would have to move fast.

They didn't. When I asked why, I was told the evidence could not be collected until it had been photographed in position.

'But by the time the photographer gets here,' I said, 'there won't be any evidence to see.'

'Sorry. It's procedure. We have to wait.'

And so we waited until the photographer eventually came and took a very expensive and highly scenic set of pictures which showed Horse Guards in winter, covered completely by a smooth, unbroken blanket of pure white snow.

I gave up on the Horse Guards situation and headed back to Whitehall. Here the search team was collecting the evidence, sweeping the road and pavement clear. I contemplated the burnt-out Transit and thought how thoroughly well-prepared this particular terrorist operation had been. Most weapons are fired by line of sight; when using a mortar, however, it is not necessary to see or be seen by a target. The bomb is lobbed high over any intervening obstacle and falls from the sky.

In order to target the Prime Minister and the War Cabinet on the morning of Thursday, 7 February 1991, the bomber had to drive into Whitehall – one of London's most sensitive areas – and park in exactly the right place and at exactly the correct angle under the very eyes of armed Ministry of Defence police on guard at buildings on either side of the road.

There was no way this could have been done by guesswork; the range and angle would have had to be calculated in advance with the aid of a large scale street map and photographs. To ensure the van was accurately positioned on the day of the attack, the terrorists had probably stuck strips of adhesive tape on the windscreen of the van. The tape would have been lined up with a predetermined point – perhaps buildings opposite – to make certain the van was in line with the target.

Witnesses reported seeing a man leaping from the vehicle shortly before the 'explosion' – before the mortars blasted skywards through a hole in the van's roof. A motorcycle pulled alongside, the man jumped on to the pillion, and the bike roared off again. The incident lasted only a few seconds; the bomber had been working with a firing system which allowed no time for error or delay, knowing full well that any vehicle which parks in Whitehall is going to be almost instantly checked by watching police.

By my calculation, the van was only five degrees or so out of line. Had it not been, then all three mortars would have hit 10 Downing Street.

1

Early Years

There would have been no reason to target Farmer Bowker's bicycle had Farmer Bowker not gone on the attack first. Shooting people just for pinching a few apples was a bit much. It wasn't as if anyone had been doing anything *seriously* wrong.

Jimmy and I had gone in quietly, carefully, weaving this way and that amongst the fruit trees. The essence of scrumping was speed: you picked the apples as quickly as you could then stuffed them inside your open-necked shirt; your trouser belt or waistband prevented them from falling out. When the front of your shirt was full, you pushed the apples around to your back, then filled the front again. Jimmy and I prided ourselves on our expertise but when we'd completed our harvest Farmer Bowker suddenly materialized, shouting, and brandishing a twelve-bore.

Running away isn't easy when you look like a Michelin Man; somehow we made it back to the boundary, bouncing and ballooning along until we reached the old wooden fence. We were astride the crosspiece when the shotgun blast split the air and pellets from the cartridge actually peppered the backs of our shirts and the apples within.

It was, we later agreed, an act of war. For honour to be satisfied some response would have to be made. Unfortunately when you're eleven years old your options for wreaking vengeance on a rural warlord are limited. So we decided to attach some rockets to Farmer Bowker's bicycle, fire them, and send the contraption hurtling across the countryside.

The idea was mooted at a council of war called in Stewart Smith's garden shed. We were, in the main, children of the camp; army kids whose home, Netheravon, housed the Small Arms School. To the north, the camp was bounded by the Salisbury–Netheravon road. Accommodation consisted of two terraces of brick-built houses, one brick-built detached, and a long row of corrugated iron huts (which, according to my mother, constituted the most uncomfortable married quarters in Britain). The operational centre lay to the east of the married quarters area. To the south stood the ammunition storage zone on ground which shelved gradually away towards the banks of the River Avon.

The camp took its name from the Wiltshire village a mile and a half away. Salisbury Plain, the vast swathe of chalk downs, spread out all around, westwards to Warminster and Westbury, north towards Devizes and the Vale of Pewsey, east towards Andover and south to Amesbury and Stonehenge. It was a wide landscape, and an ancient landscape, and a perfect place to launch a rocket-propelled bicycle.

As befitted children of military households, the operation unfolded with military precision. Intelligence was vital. The girls came in useful here: a small group of them set about a discreet surveillance of Farmer Bowker. In the meantime we attended to the fine detail. The calculation of velocities and payloads was, to us, not an unfamiliar activity. This was an era when boys usually spent their time assembling complete sets of Turf cigarette cards, albums of exotic stamps and lists of Black Five engine numbers; our interests lay elsewhere.

In my case, a preoccupation with bombs and rockets was an inevitable consequence of growing up in Netheravon. Safety procedures, though learned by heart by everyone on the camp, were rarely observed: unused ammunition was frequently left behind after training in the weapons pits. To a small boy the discovery of abandoned .303 cartridges was akin to finding El Dorado; I would break them open, extract the cordite, and use this to manufacture bangers, crackers and rockets.

More useful skills were also acquired, including the accurate recognition of 'blind' 2-inch mortar illuminating bombs (a blind is the term for any filled projectile – that is, one containing high explosive, smoke or illuminating composition – which has failed to function as intended on impact or arrival at the target). The mortar illuminating bombs contained a flare attached to a parachute; when functioning correctly, the flare would ignite and was ejected at the apex of the bomb's trajectory. Suspended from the parachute, the flare would then descend gently to earth. The parachutes were much sought after by camp children for their high barter value; even adults found uses for the cotton fabric.

But this type of munition had a high failure rate: bombs frequently fell back to earth with flare and parachute still intact because of malfunctions of the ignition and ejection system. If you knew where to look you could soon find them, for although the bombs usually buried themselves in the ground, their tail units remained visible. To a child this was a valuable but potentially deadly harvest: many hours of careful study were needed to learn the difference between useless smoke bombs, the much-prized illuminating bombs, and the lethal unexploded HE (high explosive) bombs.

As time went by I progressed to larger and deadlier bombs and became adept at removing the safety mechanisms from the fuzes of various projectiles so that they would explode when dropped on to hard ground (usually by suspending a prepared bomb from a piece of rope and then arranging for the rope to burn through).

My confidence grew, but others, particularly my mother, were not so sanguine: relaxing quietly one evening at home, she heard a heavy thump from my bedroom, hastened to investigate, and discovered me sitting on my bed practising catches with a Mills hand grenade.

'Peter! What on earth d'you think you're *doing*?'

'Me?' I stared blankly. 'I'm not doing anything. I was just throwing this up and down.'

'But it's a hand grenade!'

'I know.' Realization dawned belatedly. 'Oh. Sorry about the noise. I just dropped it.'

'You just dropped it?'

'It's all right, it's not dangerous or anything.' I smiled the smile that children display to reassure adults ignorant of the finer points of modern technology. 'Look, you can see it's empty . . .'

By way of confirmation, I began to unscrew the bottom of the grenade, certain that this informative demonstration would calm as well as clarify.

'Stop it!' Mother moved nearer, angry now. 'Get this thing out of here right now! I am not having a hand grenade going off in *my* married quarters.'

I took the grenade away and reflected, not for the first time, that though parents were all right, they were not a lot of fun.

Fun, of course, was what life was all about, and explosions were caused for the sheer joy of it; it was not our intention to harm either people or property. This meant we couldn't risk hurting Farmer Bowker, and we decided to concentrate our attention on his bicycle.

But theory was one thing and practice another. As the senior explosives expert in the group, it fell to me to construct several home-made rockets and attach them to a bicycle generously loaned by Jimmy. But though the rockets fired satisfactorily, the bicycle refused to move: we simply hadn't enough motive power to shift its mass.

This was particularly irritating because the girls had finished target reconnaissance: they reported that Farmer Bowker, who worked a section of land between the camp and the Larkhill firing range, regularly at the same time on the same day of each week cycled out to the edge of the range, left his machine behind, and went off shooting with his twelve-bore.

The operation had now taken on a painful urgency. Not only was it necessary to redeem our honour; there was the imminent prospect of being humiliated by a gang of girls. Problems were compounded because there was no guarantee that you would find what you needed when scavenging around the base.

But then we discovered a large cylindrical device out on the ranges: 4 feet 6 inches long and 3 inches in diameter, it was marked TAIL PROPELLING U3 ROCKET. It was fitted with a replica concrete warhead and appeared to be electrically initiated: two wires trailed from the venturi. Although at first sight this looked a little daunting, we'd all seen smoke generators with their attendant wires and had watched them being set off; we trusted that the rocket's ignition system would function in similar fashion.

We repatriated the U3 and lugged it across five miles of undulating downs. We hid it as near to the target location as possible, covered it with loose earth and leaves, then trudged back home on aching legs.

The day of the attack dawned like any other summer's morning, the sun climbing lazily up from the horizon, limning the dense stands of beech and horse chestnut cradling the camp. We were already in position when Farmer Bowker arrived. I peered out from between strands of meadow grass, feeling the hardness of the ground, listening to the drumming of my pulse, thinking that at any moment Bowker would hear the same tattoo and come to investigate. But after setting his bicycle down he merely hefted the shotgun and strode off towards the ranges.

One minute. Two minutes. And then we sprang from cover, dragged the U3 from its hiding place and carried it over to the bicycle. Eager hands steadied the frame while the rocket was attached, nose pointing out beyond the handlebars and wicker carrier basket, tail unit resting on the rear carrier tray. Within seconds it was lashed into place front and back; extra cable that had earlier been connected to the original venturi wires was run out, snaking back across the grass to a firing position we'd established behind a nearby concrete pillbox.

The original plan – to launch the rocket at the moment when Farmer Bowker reappeared on the scene – had had to be scrapped because none of us were sure whether we'd mastered the technique of electric ignition. If the thing didn't go off, then we'd either have to run away and abandon our prized weapon or retrieve it but risk being shot at in the process. We therefore thought it best to push the ends of the cable into the sockets of our army radio battery and see what would happen.

I don't know what we were expecting, but the explosion wasn't like anything we could have imagined. The rocket ignited in a great gout of flame, made the most appalling – and frightening – noise, and then screamed off into the sky, taking the bike with it. Thrown completely off balance by the unorthodox load, the U3's flight path abruptly degenerated into a series of agonized bounds. It managed to clear about 200 yards before smacking into the earth, shedding large chunks of the bicycle on impact, then took off into space at breathtaking speed only to screech back down and shed a few bits more. Again it bounced up, and again it crashed down, until like some strange incandescent kangaroo it finally disappeared from sight in the heart of the ranges, pieces of bicycle spraying out in its wake.

There was a moment of dumbstruck silence – I think it was silence, we were all so deafened we couldn't have heard anything anyway. Then slowly, hesitantly, we came out from behind the pillbox to survey the launch site. Where the bicycle had stood only moments before there was now just a patch of dark scorched earth. Wisps of smoke hung languidly in the air.

Later, I confessed to my father. There was no alternative: there were bound to be questions about a low-flying bicycle suddenly exploding across the Larkhill firing range. Someone would have to carry the can and, as I was the ringleader, it was me.

To my surprise, my father literally fell about laughing. He went on laughing for what seemed like a very long time. And then he gave me an Almighty Bollocking, Grade 1, concluding it by saying he would visit Farmer Bowker and offer both explanation and financial compensation.

I was amazed. 'You're going to pay for it?'

'No. You are.'

So my father regaled Farmer Bowker with a lengthy and apologetic tale of a mishap during manoeuvres; and I found myself having to meet the cost of restitution by lifting sugar beet for countless days and weekends afterwards.

According to my Birth Certificate, I was born on 12 December 1931 in Greenwich. According to my grandmother, I was born on 12 December 1931 in Limehouse. There was a world of difference between the two boroughs: trim, leafy Greenwich, a respectable suburb on the south bank of the Thames; noisy, dilapidated Limehouse, almost directly opposite on the river's north bank: a teeming outpost of London's East End. My mother registered my place of birth at her parents' address: in an era when respectability was all, Greenwich clearly made for a superior pedigree.

I remember neither Greenwich nor Limehouse from my earliest years. What I do remember are the camps, the succession of married quarters we inhabited as we followed my father's regiment from one barracks to another.

Father was an infantry soldier with the Royal Hampshire Regiment. Slim, athletic, and of average height, he had dark brown wavy hair and a moustache as trim and as rakish as Douglas Fairbanks Junior's. He called my mother 'kid'; she called him 'Ed'. She seemed to me to be tall in comparison to other mothers, full-figured, very upright of carriage and bearing. She always

walked with head held high, her movements imbued with a dignified gracefulness.

Despite its unsettled nature, family life in the different camps
and barracks was probably as good as anywhere else in 1930s
England, especially as Father was only away for short periods.
Even one of the furthest duties, Palestine, did not seem to require
a prolonged absence.

Our nomadic existence eventually ended when we moved to our
tin hut at Netheravon. The army proclaimed them to be the latest
thing in corrugated iron, but they were ugly and flimsy. Thankfully,
in time we progressed to better things: first a bigger tin hut with
three bedrooms, and finally to a house in one of the brick-built
terraces.

In its early years Netheravon was the army's Machine Gun
School and, later, the Support Weapons Wing of the Small Arms
School Corps. Finally it became the Infantry Heavy Weapons
Wing, a centre of specialist activity and a tight-knit community
itself.

Once we had settled into Netheravon I was sent to Figheldean
Infants, a two-roomed schoolhouse ruled by a small and bespec-
tacled lady called Miss Berlin. She had a presence that belied her
size and a speed that denied her age. Her energy did wonders
for one's concentration; the camp children and the village
children were united in absorbing the four Rs of reading, 'riting,
'rithmetic and retribution. The school lay two miles from
the camp; we walked there through field and woodland and over
the three bridges that spanned the River Avon and two of its
tributaries.

Spring gave new impetus to what we called the Big River, the
Small River and the Stream. The Avon quickened its pace, racing
with us as we sped along the riverbank in search of new adventures.

In summer we chased each other round narrow grassy verges of
wheat-filled fields then flopped breathlessly down, air rifle in hand,
to wait for rabbits to pop their disbelieving heads from their

burrows. We swaggered home with our treasure for 'the pot' much to the delight of our mothers.

By autumn the rabbits had learned to keep their heads down. Instead we turned our attention, and our rifles, to vermin: rats and grey squirrels whose tails brought us a one penny bounty.

Winter had little impact on our carefree lives. We cheered when snow fell hoping only that it would fall long and fast enough to leave a worthy toboggan run. It crunched underfoot as we tramped to school with light hearts and snowballs flying past our ears. Christmas came, and Christmas went, and the seasons unfolded around Figheldean, a picture-book village in an enchanted landscape.

Eventually I transferred to senior school at Netheravon, a brief and featureless sojourn that ended when I passed the entrance exam to Bishop Wordsworth's School, Salisbury. This, because it was on the register of public schools, greatly pleased my mother; it demonstrated the kind of scholastic progress to be expected of a child of Greenwich.

Salisbury was almost fifteen miles from Netheravon. Unfortunately the only means of getting there was the eight o'clock bus, a public transport renowned more for the attractiveness of its rural route than the accuracy of its time-keeping. I so often missed morning service in the school chapel that Mother began to wonder if the Wilts & Dorset Omnibus Company was seriously intent upon turning her son into a heretic.

Classes at Bishops ran only from 9.10 a.m. to 1 p.m. Such was the intensity of the teaching regime that to be even a few minutes late was to be left like a runner at the starting block while the rest of the field forged far ahead. The school day was so severely truncated because Bishops had to accommodate both its own intake and another from Portsmouth, boys who slipped into our desks in the afternoons (what they did in the mornings was and remains a mystery to me). Displaced pupils from a city under attack from the Luftwaffe, they learned in one shift and we in the other.

For war now raged, a war that was changing everything, yet which at its outbreak had meant surprisingly little to the children of the camp. The summer of '39 had been like all other summers; the world of the adult and the world of the child had continued to maintain their separate orbits. There was much to do, even on wet days, for that was when we gathered together to discuss future projects that usually never amounted to anything or to plan tree houses that most impressively did.

With the rain beating down outside it was a good time to resort to conventional pursuits, to barter carefully hoarded copies of comics such as the *Hotspur* and the *Rover*, to entertain each other with silly impressions of Tommy Handley and Dick Barton. When the sun shone again we were back outdoors, playing football according to rules that were few and simple: stay within the lines and don't hit anybody.

Though outdoor life was preferable to indoor life, of all the pleasures of that era, one was arguably supreme: going to the pictures, either at the camp or at RAF Netheravon, a three-mile walk away. The RAF had a plush and proper affair with pull-down seats, a projector that always worked and a twice-weekly programme change. By contrast our cinema existed more in spirit than substance; a giant Nissen hut normally used for lectures and training sessions, it offered but one film a week on one day a week, though disconcertingly rarely on the *same* day each week because screenings were scheduled around camp exercises. The screen flickered and shimmered and frequently managed to do no more than depict grainy white blobs against an uncertain background to the accompaniment of an equally shaky soundtrack. Intervals were frequent due to the primitive projection equipment: when a reel had to be changed, the film was stopped and the lights turned on while the projectionist frantically struggled with the spools and cogs. The film would frequently break and the 'cinema' erupt in a chorus of booing and catcalls.

The giant hut was cold, too, in spite of the two coal-fired stoves. A seat near either was to be desired, except on the occasion when someone threw a handful of 9mm cartridges into the fire and the things started popping and banging all over the place.

That summer slowly turned to autumn, and shadows lengthened early across the fields. My father was not in the British Expeditionary Force and thus remained at home; my sister Maureen, born in July 1936, had at last become interesting after what seemed an unending period of babyhood. Even the anticipated arrival of another baby sister or brother – I couldn't have cared either way; all they did was make a lot of noise and demand a lot of attention – did nothing to undermine the serenity of family life. Days of laughter were followed by nights of content, and I slept unaware of faraway death. And then, one quiet afternoon, death was no longer so distant.

The purpose of the Small Arms School was to teach infantry men to use weapons other than the traditional rifle and bayonet. Because of the war everything was now geared to getting the maximum number trained in the shortest time possible.

Speed was all: out went the practised rituals of drill parades and kit inspections, in came a new urgency, an acceleration of tempo that achieved more yet overlooked much. Safety was no longer given the attention it required; though rules were not deliberately waived, the pressure on training schedules was such as to narrow the margin between discretion and disaster. That afternoon the margin narrowed fatally.

I was going to get some flour for my mother from the NAAFI, yet another of Netheravon's ubiquitous tin huts with a canteen at one end and a shop at the other. The canteen was frequented by soldiers who could purchase everything they needed – beer, Blanco, shoelaces, cigarettes; the shop was more of a general store with a long counter, old-fashioned till and goods stocked on ceiling-high shelves. The place was popular with the thirty or so families quartered on the camp because prices were low, stock was reasonably comprehensive, and it saved you a two-mile hike to the nearest village shop.

That afternoon there was no reason to hasten, not with the sunlight still warm on the grass and the soldiers unwittingly providing an outdoor entertainment – a training session featuring the 29mm Spigot mortar, the unconventional 'Blacker Bombard'.

A conventional weapon is aimed by sighting its barrel and firing. The propellant charge ignites and pushes against the base of the projectile which then travels up the barrel and flies away in the direction of the target. Unusually, the Blacker Bombard had a spigot instead of a barrel, a machined steel rod inserted into the end of the projectile's tail tube. The propellant – a cordite charge – was contained in a cartridge at the inner end of the tube; on firing, a striker on the spigot would hit a percussion cap on the cartridge and ignite the propellant. Gases generated by the burning cordite would then force the projectile off the spigot and send it towards its intended destination. Lacking the heavy barrel and recoil mechanism of conventional weapons, the spigot type was much lighter and therefore much cheaper to manufacture. Although it also lacked range, it could accurately lob a 20-pound bomb containing 8 pounds of high explosive over a distance of around 450 yards.

I watched the soldiers as they formed a semicircle around the instructor and the Blacker Bombard. Voices carried clearly on a strengthening breeze. From their actions it seemed they were using a dummy mortar, one where both warhead and propellant were totally inert, rather than a practice mortar, where only the warhead is safe. Obviously they were rehearsing aiming and firing procedures; when they pulled the trigger, nothing would happen. The bomb was black and hooped with a yellow-painted ring. It was loaded on to the spigot. At the instructor's command, the trigger was pressed.

From my vantage point on the perimeter grass I watched with disbelieving eyes as the bomb hurtled from its spigot, the crack of its cordite charge splitting the air. The dark, frantic blur struck one of the soldiers, and threw him aside like a rag doll. It careened off into another, shredding tunic and flesh as it tore out most of his chest. It felled a third victim, then veered away towards a nearby building, slammed against the wall, bounced back, rolled over and over and lay still.

The figures remained where they had fallen. The others stood in frozen profile, matchstick men pinned into place. Inert, incongruous, the bomb lay negligently on the grass; sunlight now added a paler stripe to its bulbous form. The breeze stirred the trees around me. Into a vision of searing lifelessness, horse chestnut leaves came fluttering down like ragged stars.

Eventually I moved away, bought the flour and walked slowly home, neither thinking nor feeling.

My mother chastised me for taking so long. She chastised me again later, when the news came out that I was the boy who had witnessed the accident, that day when a spigot mortar had been mistakenly loaded with a practice round.

We sat in the reverberating gloom of the Anderson shelter, Old Bill, my grandmother and me. The rubbery smell of gas masks mingled with the dank scent of moist cold earth. Another night raid was under way; the ground shook and shuddered as bombs rained down on both sides of the Thames.

Because my mother had thought it would be good for me to get away from the dangers of the camp, I had spent part of my school holiday at my grandparents' home, arriving at roughly the same time as the Luftwaffe. Though no blame for this unfortunate coincidence could be attached to my mother, it seems strange that at a time when children were being sent out of London to safe havens throughout the English countryside, I should be evacuated from the countryside and packed off into the Blitz.

London had moved from peace to war with little fuss or drama,

at a pace so gradual yet so remorseless that what was unreal on
one day passed unremarked on the next. To a child it was very
exciting: air raid wardens, black-out curtains, streets without railings, whistles and sirens in the night; and especially the aftermath
of bombing, when spent cartridges and steel splinters from
anti-aircraft shells could be collected and, best of all from my
point of view, unexploded incendiary bombs hoarded for future
use.

None of the names and places meant much to me, but my grandmother remembered the autumn of '38: Hitler's threat of war
on 1 October if Czechoslovakia failed to return the Sudetenland,
Chamberlain's flights to Berchtesgaden and Bad Godesburg, the
high anxiety of the weekend of 24 and 25 September, the dawn of
Monday 26 September when the first sandbags appeared outside
office buildings and posters printed in big black type advised of
respirator distribution points (three sizes were available – large,
medium and small; you were measured by voluntary workers who
told you to take good care because each gas mask cost the Government two shillings and sixpence).

Everywhere, she recalled, Londoners had a new phrase: 'Just in
case', taking comfort in the fact that what was being done was
more of a precaution than a necessity. When the KEEP OFF THE
GRASS signs were removed from Hyde Park that Monday, and
civilian labourers arrived in shirtsleeves, braces and cloth caps to
dig deep trenches, it was 'just in case'. When keepers and hostesses
were photographed at Regent's Park Children's Zoo shovelling
sand into maize sacks the newspaper headlines said the same thing:
JUST IN CASE. Even when a dozen stations on the London Underground simultaneously closed, everyone said it was 'just in case';
a spokesman testified to the sudden discovery of an urgent need
for unspecified 'structural alterations'.

But then Chamberlain made a final visit to Hitler and returned
from Munich on Friday 30 September with a copy of the pact which
guaranteed that Britain and Germany would never again go to war.

'I believe it is peace in our time,' he said. 'Go home and sleep quietly in your beds.'

And now here we were, in an air raid shelter in a back garden in Greenwich, my grandfather complaining in a voice heavy with irony about how good it was to be at home, sleeping quietly in our beds.

The darkness jarred again as something thudded near by. Bright light suddenly flooded the shelter and our shadows stood out in flickering relief. Grandmother pulled me to her, shouting: 'It's an incendiary!'

Grandfather glared at her. 'I know, I know!' Pugnaciously: 'Stop yer yelling, will yer?'

'Aren't you going to do something?'

'What, *now*?' He looked at her as if she'd gone mad.

I stared from the one to the other, mesmerized by the sudden slanging match. The ground trembled again; sound came drumming as distant bombs fell. I was too old to be frightened but too young to appreciate what might happen next.

Grandmother stubbornly refused to yield. 'You've got to put it out, right this minute!'

'If you think I'm goin' out there in this,' he said, rather as one might point to the folly of setting forth in a rainstorm without an umbrella, 'if you think –'

'Oh I see, I see! Let's all just sit here and wait for the next one to drop! You know very well they use incendiaries as markers. They can see our house clear as day now.'

A momentary pause, then: 'Bloody Huns!' and he clamped his bowler hat to his head and lunged outside.

We watched him from the shelter entrance, shovelling earth on to the blazing incendiary. The first shovelful made the thing erupt in a spectacular shower of sparks; like a figure from a surreal fantasy, he hopped this way and that, frantically brushing at his shirt and trousers, all the while keeping one hand clamped to his hat.

Old Bill's bowler: the hat was inseparable from its owner. He wore it at breakfast and he wore it at suppertime and no one, not even the bloody Hun, was going to part him from it. In the neighbourhood he was regarded as a fierce old rogue, a description not entirely inappropriate. He was a self-employed plumber and used to bring home sections of lead piping which, for reasons never disclosed, he found it necessary to hide. By contrast, Grandmother was smaller, almost frail, yet each of them knew who ran the household, for her stubbornness usually defeated his bluster. If that failed, then downright guile was used.

'They need help to clear up,' she said, when one particular night raid had finally ended and volunteers were being sought in a door to door appeal.

'They can manage without me,' Old Bill said, shuffling deeper into his fireside chair. 'Some of us 'ave already 'ad an 'ard day.'

Grandmother smiled sadly. 'What a shame. They'll be wanting all the able-bodied men they can find, down at Lovibonds.'

'Lovibonds?'

'Mmmm. The brewery. It's had a direct hit.'

Old Bill briefly considered, then hauled himself out of the chair. 'I'll just get my coat,' he said.

As the war years slowly passed, and the Luftwaffe ceased to threaten London's skies, Greenwich became more and more a place for holidays, a time for staying at Grandfather's side as he laboured in his workshop or, even better, for walking together along the riverside, watching the sailing barges beating up and down the Thames.

These holidays provided a welcome break from the rigours of school life at Bishop Wordsworth's, and the interminable hours of homework. Scholastically, I was lazy; although I would eventually end up with an Oxford Schools Certificate, consistent under-achievement disappointed both my teachers and my parents.

However, where explosives were concerned it was a different story. By now I was skilled in the manufacture of weapons from various spares left lying around the camp. The most common were 9mm Sten gun barrels, which when fixed into a standard 1-inch signal pistol barrel could be used as a single shot weapon. Unfortunately they only lasted for a few admittedly hair-raising rounds, after which the material holding the Sten gun barrel in position finally failed and blew the barrel out of the gun. I lost count of the number of such weapons I managed to fabricate; I'm told that one such gun, allegedly made by me, is today on display at a Wiltshire police college.

The war was bringing finer treasure, too, notably a crate of Maschinen Pistole 43s, a German assault rifle. A brand new weapon, its arrival for evaluation at Netheravon generated a flurry of interest that was not lost on the children of the camp.

Several instructors, including my father, had an MP 43, but no one worried about leaving the weapons lying round – what little ammunition existed for them was safely locked away in the stores and could only be drawn by authorized users. I decided to make some of my own.

It took time as well as practice but eventually I modified a couple of dozen conventional German rifle cartridges to suit the new weapon. Hopeful though not certain that the ammunition would work, I purloined Father's MP 43 and then led two senior members of our gang out of the camp and across the Salisbury–Netheravon road to the firing ranges.

About 400 yards in we found a set of old trenches. We crouched down while I took aim and fired at a trench wall twenty feet away. Unfortunately, though the rifle worked perfectly, the rifleman did not: a child's strength was no match for the weapon's ferocious kickback. The barrel lifted and the rounds went over the top.

My companions were decidedly unimpressed. 'Just look at him,' said one. 'Can't even hit a bloody wall.' He reached for the rifle. 'Give it here.'

But then someone landed in the trench. 'What the hell are you lot *doing*?' White-faced, shaking, the Orderly Officer pushed us aside and scooped up the ammunition. We were so dumbfounded by his arrival that it took a few seconds for his words to register: the bullets had not only sprayed over the trench wall, they'd also gone over the road, passed through the trees in the Top Wood – clipping off leaves and branches en route – and then whistled over the camp. For a few brief moments Netheravon thought the Germans were very close indeed.

This time there were not only wrathful parents but a wrathful army to contend with. A couple of days later we were all taken before the Colonel. We had, he said, behaved in an extraordinarily irresponsible fashion. Yes, sir. We had put people's lives and safety at risk. Yes, sir. Did we now realize the seriousness of what we had done? Oh yes, sir.

Having identified me as the ringleader, the Colonel glared more at me than at anyone else. How, he enquired, had I managed to come up with ammunition for the MP 43? Haltingly to begin with, but then more fluently as his attitude seemed to soften, I explained the research and development programme that had preceded the firing. Despite himself, he couldn't quite hide his fascination. Finally he said: 'And now I've something to tell you, young Mr Gurney.'

'Yes, sir?' My face must have been bright with anticipation – after all, I had made the weapon work. That had to be *some* kind of achievement.

'We've examined your ammunition and we've rechecked the rifles. And d'you know what?'

'What, sir?'

'If you'd fired that thing just one more time it's very likely it would've blown up in your face.' The Colonel hunched forwards over his desk. His smile was humourless. 'What d'you have to say to *that*?'

I swallowed hard. I had nothing to say.

As a lesson, it was well worth the learning; certainly, it was more readily absorbed than anything at school. My affinity with

explosives should at least have stimulated an interest in chemistry,
but unfortunately the subject was taught in such a way that it was
about as fascinating as watching paint dry. Only on the playing
field did I excel: after carrying off the Victor Ludorum, I was made
School Captain of Athletics.

When Grandfather learned I was a promising sprinter he
borrowed a stopwatch and off we went for a time trial in Greenwich
Park. He paced out what he claimed to be a hundred yards and
sent me on my way. When I'd finished he was staring at the
stopwatch and shaking it. I skipped over to him. 'How'd I do?'

'Under nine seconds.' Old Bill frowned. He shook the stopwatch
again. 'Nah. Can't be. Bloody thing's obviously wrong.' But when
he looked up, he was smiling.

The war that had dawned unrecognized was now ever-present,
first in Greenwich and then in Netheravon. In June 1940 troops
evacuated from Dunkirk arrived at the camp. Exhausted, disorien-
tated, they crowded into tents. We watched and wondered at their
sallow faces and shuffling movements, at the absence of smiles and
the dullness of their eyes. They gave us handfuls of French coins.
At first the NAAFI wouldn't take them, but then relented, so we
spent our francs and centimes on condensed milk and squares of
jelly. I used to think the soldiers gave us the money because they
didn't need it any more, but as time passed I began to sense a
different reason. Eventually I understood what had been meant by
a soldier who handed me a souvenir – a leather belt to which had
been carefully stitched a line of shining centimes, the thread sewn
through the holes in the coins. 'Take it,' he said. 'I don't want
anything to remind me of France.'

We continued to live at Netheravon beyond war's end. Finally,
when I was seventeen, Father transferred to the Royal Army Ordnance Corps and was posted to the British Army of the Rhine
(BAOR). The rest of the family went with him – my mother, my
sister Maureen, and the two others whose arrival seemed to have

come out of the blue: brother John, born in November 1939, and Diane, born in January 1943.

Because it was important for me to finish school at Bishop Wordsworth's, I stayed behind in Netheravon Village, lodging with a couple whose son was at Sandhurst. Towards the end of that last term I was warned of my liability for National Service call-up and asked to state in which arm of the forces I would prefer to serve. After enquiring into the options available, I discovered that the army offered a trade as an ammunition examiner; it seemed a very interesting way of spending eighteen months. Luckily this was a Royal Army Ordnance Corps trade; I pointed out that my father was already in the RAOC, knowing full well that the selectors paid more attention to family ties than to anything else.

Eventually a brown envelope popped through the letterbox. Headed 'On His Majesty's Service', it contained orders to report to Aldershot, a postal order for one day's pay – four shillings – and a rail travel warrant. It was 25 May 1950. I was in the army now.

2
Army Life

An ammunition examiner's job calls for the exercise of specialist knowledge, an ability to act calmly and responsibly under pressure, and a facility for matters mechanical. Challenges are many and varied. Tasks are often of considerable complexity and require the display of initiative and ingenuity. So the selection board at Parsons Barracks, Aldershot, gave me a dismantled bicycle pump and asked me to put it back together again.

Each preceding test had shown the same sophistication of selection process: intelligence – a set of puzzles from 1949 Eleven-plus exam papers; psychological – a couple of pages of ink blots. And now, the bicycle pump.

It made me realize how lucky I was to have got this far, for the army's idea of sensible selection had a logic all of its own: a friend who had been one of London's best bricklayers was made a driver; another, a genius with car engines, wound up as a clerk. Yet none of this was surprising because, after my first two weeks of National Service, it was obvious that the army moved in curious ways.

Parsons Barracks comprised a series of wooden huts dotted around a grassed area and interspersed with the occasional tree. Each hut provided accommodation for thirty men in the main dormitory area; a small bedroom at one end was reserved for the permanent Staff Corporal. His job was to encourage us through our training. Accordingly, he bellowed everything at the top of his voice, rendering every command well-nigh incomprehensible.

The intake at Parsons was drawn from a wide social spectrum; it included a talkative Welshman, a taciturn Scot, an East End barrow-boy and a couple of chaps of 'quaite refained' upbringing. From Reveille to Lights Out every moment was taken up with training. After the evening meal at 1700 hours there was something called 'Interior Economy'. This involved the cleaning and preparation of one's kit for the following day: Blanco all webbing, clean all brass, press uniform, prepare bed space for inspection and 'bull' boots (bull being a verb for the act of polishing with one's finger).

In those brief exhausted moments after Lights Out there was little time to ponder on the army's strange terminology or tasks like whitewashing coal, grading pebbles – and shaving blankets. All bedding had to be folded and boxed for morning inspection. But this being the army, boxed did not mean boxed; it meant sandwiching one's neatly folded sheets between one's neatly folded blankets and then wrapping another blanket around the assembled fabric to make an aesthetically appealing pile. The exposed faces of the folded blankets were required to be free from fluff. To ensure *that*, these needed to be shaved.

Once you began to understand the thinking that informed this kind of duty, the task of arranging pebbles by shape and size or applying whitewash with a toothbrush to lumps of coal was of little consequence. The apparent aim was to mentally and physically exhaust every recruit to the point where every order, no matter how stupid, would be obeyed without question, which explained why the British army was the world's best army and why those who ran it were very probably certifiable.

After two weeks' inductions and trade aptitude selection, after seemingly endless days of saluting and marching and being treated as though one were deaf as well as retarded, we were sent to

Badajos, a barracks a couple of miles away. No one had seen it but everyone had heard ominous rumours. On a warm bright morning we marched towards the place which, for the next six weeks, we would call home. Spirits were high: we'd done two weeks, we were veterans already. Things were looking up.

Unfortunately Badajos turned out to be exactly as advertised. It reared up stark and gaunt, a three-storey, brick-built Victorian edifice decked with full-length cast-iron balconies that reminded one of the interior of some US state penitentiary. The march halted. Spirits sank. Jokes petered out. We were standing and wondering and waiting when a body flew through the air and smashed hard into the gutter.

It was, the army later said, an accident. A despairing young soldier had *not* decided to end it all by throwing himself off the topmost balcony. He had fallen, that was all.

We slept fitfully, that first night. The next day we absorbed our new surroundings. Each barrack room housed thirty men, with a small bunk room – as at Parsons – for the permanent Staff Corporal. Beds were separated by about a yard. Communal washing and lavatory facilities were provided on each floor but, as the basins were devoid of plugs, ablutions were performed with difficulty. The shortage of plugs was matched by a shortage of lavatory doors. The lack of personal privacy worried us less than the army's lack of organization: if they couldn't organize some sink plugs and a few lavatory doors, then God help them if they had to organize another war.

Indeed it was daily growing more clear that the army couldn't organize anything. On one occasion, after being instructed on how to form three parade ranks, our Training Battalion was told by an NCO that our resulting formation was 'one behind the other twice'. Soon afterwards I and another soldier were given the order: 'You two form three ranks and stand still while I go and 'ave a look for another one.'

Permanent staff NCOs tended to give orders with greater

clarity, but they took about as much interest in us as a Ford assembly-line worker takes in the bits of motor car that pass before him. We had to be of the right shape, we had to fit, and we all had to move as one when slotted together. If you were bemused or bewildered there was no chance of asking, nor much point.

By now the squad had been broken up into various groups. Grouping depended on which army trade had been deemed appropriate for each individual. For some reason most of my intake had been categorized as storemen, so they moved into Salamanca, a neigbouring barracks. I was the only one to be selected as a likely ammunition examiner and thus, for the remainder of my stay at Badajos, I trained with four potential officers – individuals whom the army clearly believed to be of superior stock.

The drill sergeant stood with feet planted firmly apart, hands clenched behind his back and an expression of fury on his face. All around, the drumming of marching feet and the brisk echo of commands eddied on the air. Everywhere else, men were being turned into soldiers. Here though, we were being turned to stone by a sergeant with a basilisk stare.

Finally his anger found voice. 'A dis-ah-star! An utter bleedin' dis-ah-star! Call yourselves soldiers? You are not *fit* to be in the Army! You are not *fit* to wear the King's uniform! You are a bigger bleedin' shambles than Passchendaele, what are you?'

It seemed best to hope the question was rhetorical. If I had to say anything now, anything at all, the words would spill out on a tide of laughter. I kept my eyes on Sergeant Crabb. It meant I didn't have to cope with the expressions on the faces of my companions: Henderson, Taylor, Williams and Clarkson.

Certainly it had been a shambles but that was hardly our fault. The problem was obvious. For company drill to take place, first you have to have a company: a company consists of three squads, and a squad consists of thirty men. Our squad, however, consisted of only four potential officers and one potential ammunition examiner. Quite how you get five men to simulate what happens when ninety men are on parade, how you school them in all the necessary manoeuvres, was beyond me.

But not to Sergeant Crabb. He had brought to the drill square five lengths of rope. One was issued to each of his five charges. He smiled in triumph as we gazed in bewilderment and even let pass unremarked Henderson's question about the flute that was supposed to play while you did the Indian Rope Trick. I hadn't said anything, inwardly debating whether this was to be some new form of torture or the Army's idea of teaching us how to knit.

But no. The ropes, Sergeant Crabb said, were not ropes at all. The ropes were soldiers.

Ah.

The ropes would take the place of the men what would 'ave been stood standin' be'ind us 'ad there been anyone stood standin' be'ind us.

Well, of course, Taylor whispered in my ear. Why hadn't we thought of this before?

Then Sergeant Crabb interrupted: 'You say something, Taylor?'

'Yes, sir. I said, er, I said we're learning the ropes, sir.'

After that, disaster was inevitable. With the ropes trailing back behind us, we endeavoured to perform steps and movements consistent with the robotic efficiency of a well-drilled parade. Unfortunately my rope tangled with Clarkson's, Williams got his wrapped around Taylor's legs and Henderson fell over his. Repeated attempts to restore order only made things worse; ropes snaked and zigzagged in all directions and mine finally developed such an affinity for Clarkson's that they welded together in a knot. Had the ropes actually represented eighty-five men, half the parade would have been hospitalized and the other half charged with indecency.

Now we were being held responsible for the manifest impracticality of Sergeant Crabb's theory. What, we wondered, would happen next?

We found out a couple of days later. Sergeant Crabb happened to mention our behaviour to a friend of his, a Guards regimental sergeant major who occasionally called into the RAOC Sergeants' Mess for a lunchtime pint. Crabb's friend offered to get us into shape. This was bad enough but worse was to come: the friend turned out to be none other than RSM Brittain, the most senior, most feared RSM of them all, a man whose reputation was known throughout the army and Civvy Street alike.

Brittain didn't so much drill us as seek to test us to destruction. We doubled this way and that, jumped to every order, winced at the wound of his staccato commands. Within a short time we were gasping for breath and perspiring freely; by contrast, he stood ramrod straight, every inch a guardsman, uniform immaculate, his pace-stick grafted to his side.

He confronted Taylor. 'You are *sweating*, soldier! Why are you *sweating*?'

'It's ... it's hot, sir.'

'*Hot?* You call this *hot?* This isn't hot. I've just come from a place where it is one hundred and five in the *shade*!'

Behind me Henderson muttered: 'Centigrade or Fahrenheit?' It was supposed to be a whisper. The RSM's smile showed that it was not.

'I think,' he said softly, 'we'd better do it all over again ...'

By the time that afternoon ended I was half a stone lighter. But at least I knew I could cope with anything now.

When the six weeks of basic training were over I was sent to 28 Battalion Royal Army Ordnance Corps (RAOC) Bramley, School of Ammunition. The army was at last ready to let me get on with learning how to be an ammunition examiner.

Bramley village was a small and sleepy community midway between Basingstoke and Reading; the camp lay on the village outskirts. It was dominated by Central Ammunition Depot (CAD) Bramley, a complex which contained so great a stock of ammunition that it extended out from the camp over an area of several square miles.

Between the camp accommodation quarters and CAD was the School of Ammunition, where ammunition examiners were taught their craft. If I succeeded in my chosen vocation, my duties would encompass all technical matters concerning munitions and explosives held and used by the British army. This included the safe storage, inspection, maintenance and, where necessary, the modification and repair of munitions and explosives. Also included was the proofing, either by firing or chemical testing, as well as the investigation of accidents and malfunctions.

There was another important area of activity: with a few exceptions, the clearance of all stray munitions and the disposal of unserviceable stocks, either by breaking down, dumping at sea or destruction with explosives.

Bramley was a turning-point in my life. It opened up fresh vistas, it brought a new and wider understanding of the science and technology of munitions and explosives, and it showed me that my childhood hobby was, in adulthood, going to be even more fascinating.

Bramley was also civilized: an expanse of lawn separated the huts – single-storey cement-rendered buildings providing fairly spacious accommodation for twenty men. All that summer the scent of newly mown grass wafted in through the open windows.

Weekends away nearly always took in the delights of London. Occasionally, though, I would return to Salisbury and visit friends. Nearing the end of my time at Bramley, I made such a journey and found myself in the company of another visitor. Her name was Daphne. Two years later she was to become my wife.

I was now a member of a genuine squad, one of a group of thirty or so trainees from throughout the UK. However, it didn't take long to discover that though the classroom was in the hands of professionals who wished only to teach their skills, the parade

ground was in the charge of the same moulders of men I had had
to endure at Badajos. Although the majority of the intake's time
was spent in the classrooms or ammunition repair workshops,
the Company Sergeant Major daily exerted his baleful presence
at the morning muster parade preceding our march to the
classrooms. Presumably the point of this was to remind us that
we were soldiers first and foremost. Morning parade was very
much an inconvenient observance of ceremony and tradition
while our heads were full of thoughts about the day's studies
and the practical work to come.

There were times, however, when some fun was called for, and
Hewitt seemed the ideal target. His high intellect was exceeded
only by his pomposity. Looking at Hewitt, you saw someone aged
eighteen going on eighty.

Being a person of regular habits and a likely future major general, Hewitt's evening schedule unfolded with military precision.
First he carefully folded his copy of *The Times*. Then he carried it
with him to the latrine block. Then he entered the cubicle and
closed the door. It was always the same procedure and it was
always same cubicle.

I don't know who had the original idea of bringing some excitement to Hewitt's dull life. A few moments before Hewitt arrived
at his cubicle, a small pyrotechnic charge was concealed behind the
overhead water cistern. By applying to the task all that we had so
far learned at Bramley, a firing system was conceived whereby the
pulling of the chain would cause the charge to go off.

Hewitt arrived and as soon as his door closed myself and others
in the plot crept into the adjoining cubicles and waited. Eventually
Hewitt ceased his perusal of the Stock Market report and pulled
the chain.

The noise of the blast racketed around the block. I leapt up and
grabbed the top of the partition, conscious not only of the rolling
echoes of the explosion but also the inexplicable sound of a river
rushing at full bore. Blown clear of its wallmountings, the cistern

was nodding up and down on its pipe while its contents emptied over the trouserless victim and his copy of *The Times*.

Urgent repairwork was now called for, but try as we might, nothing in the Bramley syllabus had prepared us for the task of mending lavatories which have sustained direct hits. Stoppages of pay for 'Barracks Room Damage' were particularly severe that week.

My first trip abroad: special troop train from London to Harwich, ferry to the Hook of Holland, then British military train eastwards across the Continent. It was December 1950. I had come second in my course at Bramley and was now on my first overseas posting, to No. 1 Ammunition Inspectorate, Headquarters British Army of the Rhine (BAOR), Bad Oeynhausen, West Germany.

Bad Oeynhausen was a spa town of stylish architecture with an atmosphere of discreet wealth. It seemed at first sight a place out of time, genteel, serene, a vision of the Europe of a different age. The hotels and many of the private houses had been requisitioned by the army to house BAOR HQ. The Ordnance Directorate, to which I was posted, was in one such former hotel, a place of high-ceilinged rooms and gilded lobby. Half a mile away my family had a requisitioned four-bedroomed house; I was given permission to live with them. With Christmas 1950 only a few days away it was a perfect time and a perfect place for a reunion.

Major Phil Froude and Warrant Officer First Class Sam Birt were highly experienced ammunition-trained officers and close friends. Phil was tall, medium build and in his mid forties. Ten years younger, Sam was avuncular in bearing and attitude, round, jolly, a cricketing fan who was much sought after as an umpire. He could do *The Times* crossword in his head and is the only person I've ever met who regularly completed the awesome *Sunday Times* Ximenes crossword.

As I settled into life in postwar Germany my perceptions of the army began to change. Here there was none of the crass stupidity which had seemed to be ingrained in military life. Instead there was a quiet professionalism. I was a part of this – watching, learning, being guided in the craft of the explosives man: conventional munitions disposal (CMD), unit ammunition inspection work, assisting with demolitions. I had a smart new uniform, with my AE's badge proudly worn on the right forearm sleeve. Although I was the most junior AE in the whole of BAOR, neither Phil nor Sam ever treated me as anything other than a colleague to be welcomed and shown consideration.

Despite their great experience and seniority, Phil and Sam were not without their sense of fun. One day shortly before Christmas, the Major called me into his office and announced, 'Mr Birt has rung up with some story about his gooseberries being tied up with detonating cord. He suggested I might like to go round and have a look and bring you along with me. It sounds suspiciously like an excuse for a Christmas drink.'

Later that afternoon we stood at the bottom of Sam's back garden, glasses of beer in hand, contemplating his gooseberries. Much to my surprise, Sam had not been joking – the bushes really were tied up with detonating cord. The cord, which looks similar to plastic-covered washing-line, had obviously been in place for several years and was now hopelessly entangled with the overgrown bushes. This, however, was no problem since, in itself, the cord is safe to handle. It is only when set off by a detonator that it explodes with frightening force and speed, about 9,000 yards a second.

Having proudly shown us the gooseberry bushes, Sam seemed content to let matters rest. Not so Phil. He finished his beer and said, 'Right, young Gurney. We can't leave Mr Birt's garden in such a dangerous condition. Get me the demolition kit.'

I watched in amazement as he connected up new detonating cord to the old and taped a detonator to it. I carried the demolition box back to the house where Sam was watching.

'Is he really going to blow up your gooseberries, sir?' I asked. Before Sam could answer, a searing flash and a gout of flame ensued and the bushes went up in smoke. The acrid fog danced and swirled; charred pieces of twig cracked and blazed all around.

Phil looked pleased. Sam looked baffled and turned to Phil. 'What,' he demanded, 'have you done to my gooseberries?'

I was still thinking about this strange episode the following week when Sam materialized at my side. 'Our Leader hath been on. Seems there's a problem with *his* garden now.'

'Gooseberries?'

'No. Not gooseberries. A Panzerfaust.'

'You're kidding, sir.'

'I kid you not.' Sam shook his head. 'I dunno, who'd be a gardener in Germany, eh?'

We arrived at the Major's quarters and made our way past lawn, shrubbery and greenhouse. The Panzerfaust lay a short distance away, half exposed in the frost-veined earth.

A shoulder-fired anti-tank weapon, produced near the end of the Second World War when German resources were diminishing and German desperation was increasing, the bomb was devoid of such luxuries as foolproof safety mechanisms. The mechanism it did have was basic: you could arm the thing merely by dropping it a yard or so on to a hard surface. The Panzerfaust contained 3 pounds of explosive; once armed, it was extremely sensitive and therefore extremely dangerous.

Sam and Phil briefly conferred. Neither of them stayed too close to the bomb. The Panzerfaust was not to be trifled with – and, in this case, certainly not to be moved. That left only one alternative: Sam would have to blow it up.

The earth erupted like a mini volcano, dirt and smoke and debris soaring skywards on a crest of bright flame. The aftershock pummelled; noise blasted in a thundercrack cacophony which drummed at ground and sky alike and then finally receded in a tinkling glissando of breaking glass.

When the smoke finally cleared Phil looked at the scene and then at Sam. 'What,' he demanded, 'have you done to my greenhouse?'

It was February 1951 and, though still on the strength of No. 1 Ammunition Inspectorate, I was now in Detmold with CRAOC 11 Armoured Division. I had a clearly defined role as Ammunition Examiner, one of a team responsible for the maintenance of the division's ammunition.

The duties appeared routine: unit ammunition inspection, demolition of unserviceable stocks and, should such a misfortune ever occur, investigation of ammunition accidents. If one went by the book, a junior NCO was not authorized to blow up anything unless under the control of a commissioned officer 'where practical'. NCOs were carefully vetted by the more senior members of the Ammunition Inspectorate. If they were found to be competent and responsible they would be given local authorization to carry out demolitions. Here at Detmold, quartered in palatial ex-Wehrmacht barracks, I had that authority. Even so, my performance was carefully monitored; I understood that I was by no means being left on my own. Still, this was my first operational posting. Lance Corporal Gurney, Ammunition Examiner, was out in the field.

The call came in late morning. After fairly mundane days of inspection and report logging, the opportunity to tackle a different kind of challenge was welcome. I readied myself for the work to come: an ammunition accident – a tank.

Two soldiers had begun loading American-manufactured 75mm white phosphorus gun ammunition into the tank. The ammunition consisted of a nose-fuzed shell loosely fixed into a brass cartridge case containing the propellant charge. One man was on the top of the tank, the other inside. The man on the top pulled the shell out of its cardboard storage cylinder and moved to pass it to his companion. The shell fell out of the cartridge case; the soldier tried to catch it but missed. It clanged off the metal surface just inside the hatch and exploded.

The two soldiers were not killed outright. The small HE charge ruptured the shell and spread the white phosphorus over the tank both inside and outside. This ignited on contact with the air, producing clouds of acrid white smoke and a fierce and terrible burning which penetrated the flesh of both men. Death was agonizing, and too slow coming.

Theoretically, the accident could never have happened. All British and American ammunition was designed to withstand the rigours of storage, handling and transportation. Safety procedures were built into every stage of the design, manufacturing and assembly process. It was impossible for the shell to detonate – unless there was something seriously wrong with its PD M57 fuze.

Artillery fuzes vary; in this case, a small brass component called an interrupter should have prevented the fuze from detonating the shell until after the shell had been fired from a gun. With thousands of such shells and fuzes currently in army use, the implications were far-ranging; either the interrupter had malfunctioned or it had never been there at all.

At the accident site the senior AE took me to one side and spelt it out. The outcome of this investigation depended on finding every last bit of the fuze, and that included the interrupter. Hopefully the interrupter would be found trapped inside the remains of the fuze body but, if not, the search had to continue until it could be stated with certainty that it had not been there.

'It will be like looking for a needle in a very nasty haystack, Gurney. Do your best,' were the AE's parting words.

As he left, a small group of soldiers who had been standing within earshot came over and joined me. They began to express their horror at what it must be like inside the tank. I started to listen but an involuntary distancing effect was taking hold, pulling me back, pushing them away. I became remote, isolated, separate from them – separated even from myself. All my thoughts had to be concentrated on the task in hand.

I was surprised when people asked me how I could be so remote, so cold-blooded. It was involuntary, instinctive – all to do with getting on with a job which required a matter-of-fact approach. What I was paid to do – and wanted to do – was to investigate and analyse the facts. No more, no less. But I would know, even as I said it, how cold it sounded, how inadequate.

Later, I was able to understand this mechanism better. It was a kind of invisible switch that was thrown at moments of maximum stress. Though senses were heightened, the switch would act as a control mechanism that filtered out emotions, imagination or memories. Objectivity was essential; anything less and the task would be denied the concentration and professionalism it needed.

When the switch snapped shut the boundary between logic and emotion was defined. Though there would always be things out there on the periphery, they did not affect me. What I saw, smelled or heard related solely to the clues and puzzles and the facts . . .

I clambered up on to the tank, manoeuvred myself inside and began the painstaking search for a tiny brass component less than 3/4-inch long and 1/4-inch wide: the needle in the haystack.

The needle was never found. Subsequent breakdown examination of other PD M57 fuzes indicated it was not the search that was at fault: the interrupter was present in the vast majority of fuzes but omitted in a few others. An oversight had occurred in production – a small omission but one with dreadful consequences.

Berlin, April 1951, and I was at Hackenfelde in the British Sector. A former German aircraft factory now housed the RAOC stores, vehicle and ammunition depots, a great sprawling complex of buildings by one of the main roads into the centre of the divided city. The ammunition facility was extensive; it had a repair workshop which would not have disgraced a base ammunition depot. It also had a senior ammunition examiner, WO1 Wallis, a Berlin veteran who used to spend some of his time on munitions clearance work in and around the city.

Six years after the end of the war Berlin was rebuilding itself
with impressive skill and at impressive speed. Though the Kaiser
Wilhelm Gedächtniskirche would remain as a gaunt and poignant
memorial, the Kurfürstendamm was back in business again with
its shops, hotels and nightclubs; trams, taxis, buses and cars formed
a dense tide of traffic from one end of the thoroughfare to the
other. Everywhere there were the sights, sounds and smells of
construction and reconstruction, giant cranes and soaring scaffold-
ing, welding and hammering, the deep bass thud of round-the-clock
pile-drivers, cement dust that clouded up from wagons and building
sites and left its gritty aftertaste hanging on the air. But everywhere,
too, there were scars and empty spaces where places and people
used to be; street corners defined by great swathes of shuttering
that fenced off one flattened area from the next; erratic ranks of
buildings whose symmetry was broken by hoardings or tarpaulins
or punctuated by wide aching gaps.

The presence of wartime munitions made any renewal project a
risky undertaking; the jaws of an excavator could as well turn over
shells, bombs and bullets as earth. For six years clearance teams
had been harvesting the streets of Berlin. There were times when
it seemed the work would still be continuing six years on.

Munitions clearance and disposal was one of Warrant Officer
Wallis's areas of responsibility. Unfortunately he had contracted
some form of dermatitis which was exacerbated by physical contact
with ammunition or explosives. Although he had acted principally
in a supervisory capacity, it was decided that another AE should
share the workload.

Accordingly I found myself in one of the echoing hangars of
Hackenfelde, meeting for the first time the group of civilian operatives hitherto in Wallis's charge. They had all been in the German
armed forces, all were highly experienced, and all obviously
wondering what this young, fresh-faced British army NCO was
doing in their midst.

My orders had been unambiguous: as far as these civilians were concerned, these *Feuerwerker*, I was in charge. As far as I was concerned, however, things were not so clear-cut. I didn't lack self-confidence – I had been thoroughly trained and I'd been involved with munitions in one way or another since childhood – but these people had racked up the kind of experience I couldn't hope to match. To simply announce that I was 'in charge' would be bloody silly.

The leader of the group regarded me with a frank, unwavering stare. I had to clarify the position for everyone's benefit. I raised my voice, hoping it would carry above the background noise of the hammering from the ammunition workshop. 'I know you've all been working with Warrant Officer Wallis. And I know you've all done a very good job. Nothing's going to change just because I'm here. I'm not replacing Mr Wallis. I'm not planning on altering anything. As far as I'm concerned, I'm here for one reason only.'

The group leader smiled. 'To take charge?'

'To learn.'

'Learn?'

'Yes. I wouldn't presume to show you what to do. But I'd appreciate it if you'd help me with what *I* have to do.' I paused, wondering if the message was getting through. 'I've been trained. I've done a fair amount of work already. But I need to know a lot more.'

Slowly: 'You wish to ... learn?'

'Yes.'

The German looked from me to the other *Feuerwerker* and back again. Finally: 'My name is Karl.' He smiled again, more certainly this time, and extended his hand towards me. 'Welcome to Berlin.'

They took me at my word. Day after day we loaded up the Bedford truck or one of the Jeeps and headed out into the city. Though many of the jobs posed no problems there were always one or two that challenged both expertise and ingenuity. The workload was heavy; even with two or more teams operating, there was a permanent backlog of non-emergency tasks.

The *Feuerwerker* were always careful, always methodical, operating like skilled professionals. I joined in the discussion, planning and execution, carried out various tasks under Karl's watchful eye, or stood aside and looked on while new and complex operations were undertaken involving devices I hadn't previously encountered. Gradually I absorbed the details of every incident, deriving satisfaction, exhilaration and gratitude at the good fortune that had brought me here.

In the coffeeshop off the Ku-damm Karl finished his plate of Bratkartoffeln (sautéed potatoes) and reached for a slice of the Black Forest Kirschtorte. I'd already eaten mine; it was like nothing I'd ever tasted before. Berlin might be divided, it might still be suffering postwar shortages in certain types of goods, but the street corner pubs and the pastry shops and cafés held within them the kind of delights that would have been incomprehensible across the Channel.

'So,' said Karl. 'You learn fast. You like this job?'

I nodded. 'I also like Berlin.'

'*Ja.* It's a good city. Maybe one day . . .' The sentence hung unfinished; you didn't need to ask what he was thinking. A Berliner by birth, he would have childhood memories of his city before the bombs fell, before the tanks and the troops swept in. He patted his pockets and extracted a pack of cigars. I had to smile to myself. In England I hadn't come across that many cigar-smokers. Here though, cigars seemed part of the staple diet.

'Anyway,' Karl said. 'You are ready. We let you loose on Berlin, eh?' He grinned. It was a private joke between the two of us; he knew I didn't need any civilian's permission to carry out my duties. But this little game gave the *Feuerwerker* a sense of self-respect and allowed me to learn more than could be gained from any classroom or workshop.

Karl took another puff on the cigar. 'You do me a favour though.'

'What is it?'

'Try not to knock down any more of my city.'

There was another job to go to, non-urgent, non-threatening, one of the dozens still stacked up despite every effort to reduce the total. The problem was that here in Berlin not only were you up against new difficulties every day, you were also up against the clock; some weeks it seemed that for every incident successfully dealt with, two more were demanding response.

I was acutely conscious of the time that was spent on certain kinds of operation. It seemed to me that we couldn't go on doing everything by the book: there had to be some incidents where safe short-cuts were appropriate. Blind mortar bombs, for instance. Time after time we were called out to deal with these and on arrival would find that only the tips of the fins were visible. You couldn't see anything else and you couldn't get at the damn thing. You had to dig down carefully, scoop out soil and stones, and finally expose the bomb body. After that it was standard procedure: you placed a charge next to the body and detonated it.

In situ destruction was insisted upon for three very good reasons: First, the relatively small amount of high explosive found in land service munitions meant that it was normally possible to protect surrounding property when destruction occurred. Secondly, projectiles normally suffer some physical damage when fired and vital components such as fuzes become impossible to remove. Third, but by no means least, fuzed projectiles which have been fired but have failed to detonate at the intended time are inherently unstable: they can go off at the slightest movement.

Artillery fuzes contain safety devices which react to the pressures and forces occurring at and after firing. Those forces are tremendous: the pressure generated in a chamber on firing can be from 1,000 to 6,000 bar; the acceleration of a shell up the barrel can be anything between 10,000g and 35,000g; the shell can be spinning at between 500 and 4,000 revs per minute. Components designed to react to such pressures include detents: under the pressure of acceleration they overcome the resistance of their springs and slide to the rear of the fuze. In so doing, they can clear the way for bolts which, acting under centrifugal force, move to bring detonators and strikers into line.

By the time a shell arrives at its target, all safety devices should have been rendered inactive. In the case of something designed to explode on impact, when contact is made with a hard surface the striker will be driven into the detonator, which then detonates the main filling.

But theory is one thing and practice another; projectiles fail to explode on impact for many reasons. But if something travelling at several hundred metres a second has collided with a hard surface and failed to explode, then it is not safe to handle.

This meant that whatever kind of blind projectile you found, shell or mortar, movement was highly ill-advised and, unless circumstances overwhelmingly ruled against it, *in situ* destruction was the norm. In the case of a blind mortar, you cleared the earth or any obstruction around the bomb and then fixed the charge.

Such exertion was acceptable when there was something to show for it. Annoyingly, though, you could spend what seemed an eternity out in the biting wind and rain and, at the end of it all, come up with nothing more than a harmless tail unit, the remains of a bomb which had exploded long ago. Valuable time had been lost for nothing.

So when the next call about a possible blind mortar bomb came in I threw some extra gear into the Jeep and raced out to the location, ready to put into practice the new Gurney Mk I bomb disposal theory. It was eminently practical, safe, and would substantially reduce incident attendance time.

The mortar was not much more than a glint in the earth. On all sides the land stretched away in a soggy expanse; no buildings near by, no people, just another of Berlin's empty acreages. I dusted some dirt off the fin-tip, then walked back to the Jeep, started her up, and navigated a way through the peaks and hollows of the site to a point about fifty yards from the suspected bomb.

I dug out sufficient soil to expose one of the holes in a fin and unrolled the electric cable I'd brought with me from the depot, tying one end through the hole, and running the rest of it across the ground and fastening it to the back of the Jeep. Both knots were secure; as soon as the Jeep moved off, the cable would take the strain and gradually tug the mortar out by its fin. It beat digging holes any day.

The engine started and I crunched into first gear, then eased back on the clutch while carefully feathering the accelerator. The Jeep rocked slightly, the vibrations running through its frame. More pedal pressure, and with infinite slowness it began to move forwards. One foot covered . . . two foot. I turned back in my seat, the better to see the bomb.

But there was no progress. The cable was now taut but the bomb was still stuck. More gear crunching, more engine clattering; the Jeep edged forward. I looked back again: nothing. This made no sense at all because (a) the bomb's mass simply couldn't withstand this kind of pressure, (b) I had already scooped some of the retaining earth out of the way, and (c) the standard army issue El electrical cable was still firmly connected at both ends. Unfortunately it was also possessed of one other characteristic which I hadn't appreciated: elasticity.

I pressed the accelerator more firmly and the Jeep moved forward. I clung one-handed to the steering wheel while poised half-turned towards the mortar.

And then at maximum extent, the electric cable suddenly contracted in on itself, the tension snapping back in a furious recoil that sent it looping high into the air. For a couple of dumbstruck seconds I stared skywards as the cable whipped like a long black lash, its tip hurtling downwards and straight towards the Jeep. Two things registered simultaneously: the cable was still attached to the tail fin; and the tail fin was still attached to the intact and unexploded bomb.

I threw myself into the well of the jeep, expecting a direct hit.

Pain exploded inside my head amidst the ear-splitting noise of the mortar going off. The Jeep lurched and stalled as mud and other debris rained down from above. The echoes dinned on for a very long time.

Eventually I clambered out and stood weak-kneed and coughing in the faint fog-like wraiths of smoke still eddying from the blast. The mortar had impacted about thirty yards from the Jeep, as evidenced by a newly created hole in the earth.

Comprehension slowly dawned as the smoke cleared away. I had not, after all, sustained a direct hit by my own bomb on my own head, though it felt like it. All I'd actually done was brain myself on the dashboard.

I got back into the Jeep and restarted the stalled engine. The pain had receded now but the headache was obviously going to continue for quite a time; already there was a lump the size of a duck egg. God knew how I was going to explain it away.

I had another close shave when called upon to deal with a Panzerfaust. This one had been found on a building site within earshot of the clanking of the U-Bahn city railway. The area was strewn with rubble and little remained of the original buildings.

The Panzerfaust appeared to have been fired because it was without its launcher tube. It lay shining dully in the weak sunshine, a small scree of stones threading in frozen tributary past its flanks. The earth was newly turned; the excavator stood near by, silent, engine switched off. Years of experience of Berlin's building sites had taught the construction crews all about the risks of working in an environment which had once been an urban battlefield.

I moved away from the Panzerfaust as carefully as I'd approached it and told the crew leader to move his people as far away as possible. As soon as everyone was out of range I prepared a small explosive charge and carried it back to the bomb, placing it alongside, but not touching, the warhead. I checked that the area was still clear and lit the fuze, then walked to safety – walked, not ran: you never ran because if you tripped and injured your leg or ankle you'd have no chance of getting back to the fuze to extinguish it nor of crawling out of range.

I stepped gingerly across the rubble. Thirty yards ahead was the remnant of a house wall, about nine feet high and pretty solid-looking. It would be a useful thing to hide behind when the explosion occurred: the blast itself wouldn't injure at that range but you could get cut by flying debris. I moved around to the other side of the wall, crouched down and waited for the distinctive crump of the explosion – at which point the entire universe seemed to split apart. The blast wave smashed against the wall and sent the entire structure keeling over and down. One minute I was in daylight, the next in violent darkness, sprawled flat under the weight of a mass of brickwork.

The wall should have fragmented as it fell, but disintegration was only partial; it pinned me beneath it while the world shook and shuddered as the thunderclap rolled on. Secondary thuds, bangs and crashes rang out because of all the stuff now coming down from the sky. Like some terrible hail, it pummelled the brickwork above me, smashing and splintering and cannoning off. And then silence.

I managed to struggle out from under the wall, stiff and shaking and wincing at the bruises but otherwise intact. I looked at the brickwork and sent up a prayer of thanks to whoever had learned to build things so carefully and so well. Red dust still danced on its surface. Fresh pock-marks made it look as though it had just been machine-gunned.

I stared at the place where the Panzerfaust had been. The hole was very large, very impressive, and totally bewildering. I reached the rim and looked down, shaking my head again. Had one Panzerfaust really done all this?

In amongst the debris and the tendrils of smoke that still drifted upwards, other fragments and shapes began to appear – something twisted over there ... something cylindrical and split wide-open over there ... All over the place, in fact: the remains of launcher tubes ... and other bits of wreckage too: the black splintered shards of mud-stained, blast-scorched packing cases, slivers of timber scattered like needles.

I hadn't blown up one Panzerfaust. I'd blown up a whole nest of precious munitions hoarded by German soldiers during the battle for Berlin – a cache that had been hidden deep and then left behind, either because those who buried it had been forced to flee or because they had been buried themselves.

The action of time upon the soil, the shifting of earth by the excavator, a variety of factors had all conspired to bring to the surface a solitary Panzerfaust, the tip of an iceberg unseen and unexpected.

That night I encountered Karl, going home from the depot. He was his usual self, happy to be going off to his family. 'A good day?' he asked.

'Sort of.'

'You learn more today?'

'I learn a *lot* today.' I grinned and waved him on his way. I didn't feel like going into it just yet. But a lesson had been learned that was not, so far as I could recollect, in any of the textbooks: if you can't check what's underneath that which you're about to blow up, then the steps that you take in connection with disposal must always be bloody great big ones.

Christmas found me far from the noise and the bustle of Berlin, in an ancient landscape of fields and farms and villages. Walsrode in North Germany – my final National Service posting.

354 Ammunition Depot was an ex-Wehrmacht complex and, in 1951, although the majority of the ammunition stored there was British, there was also an appreciable stock of Wehrmacht ammunition. This had been retained since much of it contained highly prized elements such as the tungsten-carbide cores of armour-piercing shells. Far too valuable to dump at sea or destroy by

demolition, the ammunition was separated into its component parts
and the non-explosive material then salvaged.

Refurbishment and repair work was carried out in a collection
of workshops which together comprised the Ammunition Repair
Factory. One of them was a hellish place – hot, crowded and noisy,
filled from floor to roof with strange devices. It was the place where
certain kinds of ammunition, some ex-battlefield and apparently
unsalvageable, were repaired and restored. Presiding over the factory's operations was Captain Scott, a small and dapper white-
haired man not renowned for his sense of humour.

Scott was one of the best engineers in the business. Within his
workshops, old munitions found new life. Dangling down from
overhead tracking, shell casings moved this way and that, dipping
into cleansing, neutralizing and phosphate baths, then swinging
out through automatic painting booths where mists of spray turned
them factory fresh.

Scott was among the last of my National Service teachers. He
taught me how to handle sausages and I learnt how to handle
German girls. Both were to prove a headache, particularly the
sausages.

Nobel's 808 explosive contains a painfully high percentage of
nitroglycerine – painful because nitroglycerine is absorbed through
the skin and breathed in from the air. The result is the worst kind
of headache imaginable.

I sat in a separate little workshop, a small enclosed space with
a chair, a bench and a sausage machine. It was actually more
complicated than that but the principle was the same: you fed stuff
in at one end and it came out in chunks at the other. The stuff was
Nobel's 808, in 50-pound lumps. I was supposed to turn it into
4-ounce cartridges: the sausages. At the end of this task I felt
like death: NG Head, as it's called, is something which, once
encountered, is never forgotten.

The girls proved to be a headache of a different kind. Sixty
of them were employed in small arms ammunition sorting and

repacking. I was put in charge. It was soon obvious to them and to me that I'd had no experience at all of running a female workforce: they giggled, they laughed, they made jokes amongst themselves which more often than not seemed to be about me.

My understanding of German was inadequate and I was beginning to feel like a schoolboy again. Clearly this couldn't go on; I had to start exercising my authority. So I began going out with Fräulein Mitzi. Mitzi was neither big nor buxom but slim to the point of angularity. She had dark hair and brown eyes and an aura of self-confidence that marked her out as a natural leader. Short of working my way through all sixty of the girls, making friends with Mitzi seemed the best solution; we would go for evening walks in the countryside or meet at local taverns. To my delight, my tactics worked well. Mitzi not only made things much easier for me in the workshop, she also rapidly improved my knowledge of German.

Off-duty hours were also spent with Davitt, Fussell, Bennett and Carroll, four others on the Walsrode complement. If we had a favourite pastime, it was tracking down the region's *Schützenfeste*, the three-day 'shooting festivals' which were so much a part of village life. Ostensibly, the object of the event was to celebrate the village's traditional shooting skills; more usually it seemed to be a fine excuse for a weekend of beer-drinking on an epic scale. The Germans were superb hosts: warm, welcoming, friendly, filled with good humour even when they weren't filled with beer.

During our time at Walsrode we learned about the fortunes that had been built up by soldiers who recognized in the old Wehrmacht ammunition the potential for private enterprise. The scale of such enterprise was not lacking in ambition: one warrant officer was caught shipping out ammunition by the train-load. He turned up for his Court Martial in a chauffeur-driven Mercedes.

Unauthorized repatriation of German war *matériel* was not solely confined to Wehrmacht ammunition nor to any one depot: another warrant officer made the fortuitous discovery that many who spent their time above the snow line were dependent on wooden skis, and that skis needed regular waxing. His depot, by chance, held large stocks of beeswax, formerly used in the manufacture of certain types of munition. The WO organized an entire ammunition workshop to repackage the beeswax into containers for sale to the skiing fraternity.

While I didn't necessarily approve, the new postwar mood of greater opportunity was encouraging. If it wasn't ammunition then it was beeswax. And if it wasn't beeswax then it was something else – petrol, for instance. Part of the war reserves of petrol were stored in the British Zone in an underground tank, a truly vast subterranean construction guarded by day as well as by night. Each guard detail spent a week at a time at the location, then handed over to the relief duty. However, before the handover could be completed, the seals on the tank's filler caps had to be examined by the incoming guard and the level in the tank monitored by a dipping rod. It was a foolproof system, and it worked perfectly for month after month: the petrol, worth a fortune on the black market, was always at the same level. The war reserve was safely intact.

Until, that is, quality control scientists discovered otherwise: brought in to check the consistency of the contents, they found that the petrol had entirely disappeared. They sampled the petrol through the usual dipping inlet, then went off to a different area of the tank and dipped that. Inexplicably, the first dip showed a full tank whereas the second showed an empty one. Examination of the prime dipping inlet revealed that it wasn't an inlet at all. Someone had at some time fashioned a tube which fitted precisely into the top of the inlet and extended down to the bottom of the tank. For months the British army had been mounting guard on a tubeful of petrol.

The culprits were never found. The thousands upon thousands of precious gallons had long since flowed through the European black market. Those involved in the operation would probably not want for money again.

Awareness of episodes such as this slowly led me towards an appreciation of interesting facets to life in the modern army. What I was interested in was a kind of life where challenges were mental as well as physical. Those early days at Parsons and Badajos had positively discouraged the exercise of intellect and had hammered all individuality out of the new recruit.

Now though, as I neared the end of National Service, it was becoming clear that the army was anything but the one-dimensional edifice it had once appeared to be. I was being trained to think and act for myself by people like Phil and Sam and Karl – all of them, in their separate ways, professionals. On the athletics track I was winning army medals and army cups; away from work, away from the track, I was enjoying the company of army friends. Setting aside the inexcusable idiocies of induction and basic training, it was clear that I was part of an organization where the living was good and could only get better; where I would meet challenge and satisfaction; where my knowledge and skill could grow. Did I really want to give all this up?

In June 1952 I signed on as a regular soldier. I returned to the School of Ammunition, Bramley, and sat in on lectures covering subjects which had been omitted from my National Service Ammunition Examiner's course. However, before I could sit the examination to become a regular army Ammunition Examiner, there occurred an army-wide AE upgrading, another examination open only to those AEs with practical experience. As I had two years' such experience I was eligible for this exam as well.

When the time came, I passed both examinations. My records – which were to cause lasting confusion to the army bureaucracy – showed that I became an Ammunition Examiner Class 2 and an Ammunition Examiner Class 1 on the same day.

3

Desert Demolitions

═══

Skeletal rather than thin, weatherbeaten rather than suntanned, with a propensity for being drunk rather than sober, Frank Wiggins was a sergeant to whom the army was both home and family. His age was indeterminable; he looked like a centenarian in the early morning but half that in the early evening. The beer bar was indeed restorative.

The Medical Officer had made things very plain less than a week earlier: if Wiggins did not confine himself to just two bottles of Allsops lager a day, then Wiggins would be recommended for discharge on medical grounds. The issue was not open to debate.

'It's bleedin' well come to somethin' when a bleedin' MO don't know the first bleedin' thing about anythin',' Wiggins confided.

I squinted against the glare of the Egyptian sun and wished Wiggins would move into the shade where I could see him better. 'What things, Frank?'

'People. About treatin' people. Don't he know the difference between one who 'as got a Medical Condition an' one who 'asn't?'

'He certainly thinks you've got a condition all right.'

'Bollocks. He just thinks I drink too much.'

'There you are then.'

'Yeah but ... he don't appreciate *why*. And he couldn't care bleedin' less either. I have to drink on account of dehydration.' He seemed to savour the word. 'Dehydration. Is that or is that not a Medical Condition?'

'Perhaps you could try water ... ?'

'I'm allergic.' Wiggins flapped an arm as though to embrace the shimmering scene of tents and huts and high wire fencing. 'Pox-ridden dump like this, a bloke dies without his liquid intake. It's bleedin' obvious.'

I shrugged. There was no point in saying anything which would extend the conversation. I made to step aside, hoping that Wiggins would get on with whatever he was supposed to be doing. Instead he grabbed my arm. 'You ever notice, the MO looks just like Rommel?'

Wiggins walked away, his shorts flapping around matchstick legs. No, I'd never thought the MO looked like Rommel. It took a Desert Rat to come up with an idea like that, not an AE Class 1 who'd landed in Egypt but a few months before.

9 Base Ammunition Depot, Abu Sultan, Canal Zone, was arguably the biggest British ammunition depot in the world. It held so much stock it took forty-five minutes just to drive around the perimeter. I had arrived here in August after an eight-month posting at 3 BAD, Bracht, BAOR. Prior to that, two years had gone by with No. 1 Independent Ammunition Company, Kevelaer, BAOR. Neither posting had been especially interesting. At Kevelaer, on the German–Dutch border, I had assisted in the setting up of an emergency ammunition sub-depot and thereafter stayed on as Senior Ammunition Examiner. As for Bracht, it had been very much a paper move; I continued to spend a lot of my time in Kevelaer.

November 1952 found Daphne and me shivering in a church where the vicar almost incinerated himself by standing with his surplice too close to a portable paraffin heater. Afterwards we all trudged out into the snow-covered churchyard and came near to freezing to death while waiting for the wedding photographer. He never arrived and we never got any pictures: we later heard he'd fallen off his motorbike trying to negotiate a snowdrift.

In the spring of 1953 I and some colleagues worked on in Kevelaer making an atomic bomb – well, one which resembled it: the task actually called for the preparation of a Nuclear Attack Simulator, something which would look impressive without necessarily wiping out a large chunk of Europe. (It worked well, too, once we'd sorted out the recipe: take 60 pounds of plastic explosive, three 50 gallon drums of napalm, bring together and then add 200 white phosphorus grenades. Though the mixture broke every rule in the book, it proved immensely satisfying: a massive bang, vast arcing sprays of white smoke and an enormous mushroom cloud that rolled high above the Hohne ranges.)

Two more years of working in Germany finally proved enough; it was now 1955 and home was an arid stretch of scrub, sand and soil in a corner of the Middle East, a depot about to be greatly reduced in size prior to handover to the Suez contractors and the departure of the British armed forces from the Canal Zone.

9 BAD, Abu Sultan, was known as a 'hard' posting, a place unsuitable for women, children, or anyone of a nervous disposition. It had an outer perimeter fence of barbed wire three yards high, a median seven-yard-wide sanitized zone, and an inner fence with searchlight and weapon tower every 400 yards. It was guarded by a full company of British Infantry and a battalion of East African troops and was targeted both by nationalist terrorists and local thieves. It had enough munitions to make a hole big enough for another canal and enough hard-living soldiers to make the closure of the beer bar an exercise which the Orderly Sergeant declined to undertake unless accompanied by at least four members of the guard.

Three days after our encounter Wiggins found a way to treat his dehydration within the terms of the MO's orders. Amidst the junk that piled up on the bar was an Allsops' advertising display, a ragged cardboard affair housing a pair of promotional bottles at least three times the normal one-litre size. Wiggins seized them with a whoop of triumph, had them filled to the top, drank both then staggered off to bed.

The wooden huts which housed the senior NCOs' bunks were set out in the form of an H. Wiggins' bunk was in the left-hand leg. Stupefied on Allsops, he went to the right-hand leg instead. The right-hand leg housed the RSM. Wiggins burst in. The RSM switched on the light. Seeing the RSM in what he thought was his own bed, Wiggins waved an admonitory finger, saying, 'Now now, sir. You know I'm not that sort of bloke.'

We heard the yelling all round the base. Peering out from our own tents and huts, we spotted an almost horizontal Wiggins in the arms of two sergeants being hauled rather than marched to the guardroom, with the RSM in shorts and vest striding furiously alongside screaming, 'Left, right, left, right,' as Wiggins' feet trailed uselessly behind him, bumping and thudding over the sunbaked earth.

My first task was to inspect the depot's extensive stocks of Mines Anti-Tank Mk 7. This type of mine contained 20 pounds of high explosive and a fuze which was held in a central cavity in the upper face. Access to the cavity (the fuze well) was via a screw-top cover plate. The mines were perfectly safe to store because the fuze was always held in an inverted position within the fuze well. You could only use the mine after it had been armed: you unscrewed the cover, removed the fuze, turned it the other way around, then placed it back inside the fuze well.

Though the mine hadn't been in service very long, reports had soon come in of a malfunction, an assembly fault which trapped a component inside the fuze and made it sensitive to all manner of stimuli. As a result, some fuzes were going off within mines held in storage. The fault was not particular to any one lot or any one manufacturer; it became increasingly obvious that a significant percentage of the army's total stock could be affected by the 'trapped needle disc fuze' phenomenon.

Given the sheer quantity of stock held at Abu Sultan, the task of checking for trapped needle disc fuzes was time-consuming. But it was not inherently dangerous: the mine could not detonate while the fuze was inverted. Every mine was safe to handle because every fuze was safely assembled in the storage position.

Until now. Now warnings had been sent out that mines had been found at another depot with their fuzes in the armed position. An army-wide alert was under way.

As the days passed, information poured in. Army statisticians reckoned that the likelihood of a trapped needle disc fuze being inadvertently assembled in the armed position was only 1 in 100,000. I didn't know how many Mk 7s were held by RAOC worldwide, but here at 9 BAD we had 300,000 of them.

If just one defective fuze went off in the armed position, then it would detonate every other mine in the same location. The only solution was to carefully unpack each mine, remove the fuze and then pack each separately and store them well away from each other. And the only way to do *that* was to resort to a bunker which, if anything went wrong, would protect those on the outside by containing the blast inside. I was the one in the bunker.

The boxes came in one by one with the mines two to a box. Sand-filled ammunition cases had been used to create the bunker; now, fenced in on all sides, my only contact with the outside world was via the blast traps – two hinged safety shields that functioned like heavyweight cat flaps.

I concentrated on my mini-assembly line, the heat inside the confined space sending rivulets of sweat across my skin. The boxes were passed to me through one of the flaps; I opened them, unpacked the first mine, unscrewed the fuze well cover plate, removed the fuze, then unpacked the second mine and repeated the procedure. That done, I passed the mines and the fuzes out through the other flap.

I had already worked my way through thousands of the mines before the alert, but it was different now. Even if a fuze functioned while you were holding it, you would be unlucky to lose more than a couple of fingers – but 20 pounds of high explosive detonating was a different matter. Everything now had to be done slowly, deliberately and more precisely. There were no odds and there were no certainties in a situation like this. The tenth mine, the hundredth, the thousandth; statistically, any one of those could be in a highly dangerous condition. But so too could be the next one out of the box. Or the one after that. You wouldn't know until the cover plate was removed.

For hour after hour the operation continued, until the heat was intense. No sound except the grating of the cover plate as it turned upon its thread. The task had its dangers but it was also excruciatingly boring and, paradoxically, I found myself hoping to discover fuzes in the armed position.

At the end of the first day they were all OK. At the end of the second day they were all OK. On the morning of the third day I rechecked the remaining stock levels. The storage locations were primitive but effective: sand sites covered with light roofing and surrounded by a substantial earth traverse, all of them well away from the operational centre of the base. One of the sites was at the very perimeter of the depot, separated from the Suez Canal by only a few hundred metres of scrub and sand. The canal couldn't be seen because of the depth of the cutting through which it ran. But a great white liner, its superstructure gilded by the early morning light, moved steadily and silently into view. Monumental, majestic, it sailed onwards across the sand.

I turned back to the storage site. The temperature was climbing; after being cooled by the velvet dark of an Egyptian night, the land and everything in it was once again experiencing the heat of new day.

Crack! Muffled, yet near; faint, but distinct. And again – *crack!* Deep within the mines' stack, two trapped needle disc fuzes went off.

By the time the work was finished, around a hundred defective fuzes had been found, the majority still intact but a number showing signs of having gone off while still in storage. No trapped needle disc fuzes were discovered in the armed position.

I was delighted to be free of the bunker, to be out in the open air again. I wasn't alone. Making my way back to the accommodation huts, I saw a familiar figure, someone last seen being dragged away to the guardroom.

Sergeant Wiggins had survived. Despite the breach of orders, the Medical Officer had decided to give him another chance. Wiggins beamed at me. 'It's like I always said, innit? The old MO, he knows what he's doin'. Right?'

The time was drawing near for our departure from the Canal Zone. There was much to do because it was not economical to shift the bulk of 9 BAD's stocks to another depot. Accordingly, large-scale demolitions became routine – operations made easier by the use of large numbers of aircraft bombs left in Egypt by the RAF and normally destined for dumping at sea. These bombs made convenient demolition charges in the destruction of other munitions which, because they contained only relatively small amounts of explosive, were difficult to detonate.

Large-scale demolitions took place miles into the Sinai, at a remote location where huge pits grew deeper with each successive explosion. All around, the land stretched away, empty of everything but a kind of sun-bleached tumbleweed that bowled along in the wind. The only cover available was a small mound a couple of miles from the pits. From here I watched the explosions, the blast wave from the detonation travelling towards me like a ripple in the surface of a pond.

Nearer the camp was an area where surplus or unserviceable propellant (cordite) was burnt. Bags of the stuff were laid out in a huge carpet and ignited by means of a long tapering propellant trail. The trail would begin at the widest point of the carpet then taper down to a single stick. Great care was needed to ensure that it would burn into the wind and that the propellant used in the trail was not the kind which would fly off in all directions once it caught fire.

Propellant burns are always impressive and, if you're out in the open, always intimidating. On more than one occasion as I watched the main carpet catch fire and the wall of flame get bigger and bigger and nearer and nearer the thought occurred that I was far too close, that this time I'd also be going up in smoke. But then, before I took to my heels, the flames would suddenly recede and die down. I would sagely nod and compose my features in such a way as to suggest that what had happened was all quite routine. Friends who have been in the same situation tell me they experienced similar feelings. We've all looked back and thought how easy it would have been to retire to a safe distance – and then doubled that distance. But none of us ever did. Moths are not the only creatures to be captivated by the flame.

I had begun work on a series of trials on behalf of the Explosives Storage and Transport Committee, which formulated the regulations governing the safe keeping of munitions. The purpose of the trials was to put some of the theory into practice; a key test was explosive wave propagation analysis.

A primary stack of munitions would be constructed and then surrounded by secondary stacks all built at varying distances from the primary. Each stack would contain only one type of munition although this could vary from stack to stack. The primary would usually consist of either Artillery Shell or Mines Anti-Tank Mk 5. The nett explosive content of the primary was around 10 tons when mines were used, a little less with shells.

The anti-tank mine was useful when observation was being made of blast effects alone. It was little more than a circular biscuit tin filled with TNT and there was minimal fragment hazard when it detonated. By contrast, shells generated a considerable number of fragments; they were used when observing the likely effect of a fragment attack.

The primary stack would be detonated and the effects of this on the other stacks noted. Occasionally, one or more of the secondary stacks would explode en masse with the primary stack; more often than not though, the blast wave would merely blow them over.

The real problem came with the shell: notwithstanding the images created in countless war movies, it is far from easy to get a stack of shells to go off simultaneously. Though the fragment strikes on the secondary stacks would frequently cause a fire, what followed next could be one big bang or a series of sporadic explosions, depending on the type of munition in the secondaries. Not only that: damaged but unexploded ammunition could be hurled hundreds of yards when a stack partially erupted; it had to be located and destroyed as quickly as possible.

I organized the final explosive wave propagation trial shortly before we left Egypt. The primary stack was composed of shells which blew cleanly and noisily, sending a blizzard of fragments whirling into the other stacks. After the smoke had cleared from the secondary explosions, I drove across the site in the company of Geoffrey Biddle, a major who had been in overall charge of the operation. The focus of our attention was what appeared to be a quietly smoking stack of mines – a secondary which, though riddled by shell fragments, had not detonated. We examined the stack carefully, the Major taking notes while I photographed the scene. Now that we were close in we could see a fire within the stack; flaming gushers of molten TNT were pouring out through the holes caused by fragment damage.

Suddenly the noise of the fire changed in pitch and intensity. I didn't need to look twice and nor did the Major: we knew that this was the sign of impending detonation. We sprinted away, heads down and legs pounding, running flat out for the Major's Land Rover parked about fifty metres away. We set off together and kept in step together and fetched up together in a tangle of arms and legs behind the steering wheel, managed somehow to get the thing started and hared off across the desert.

Finally the Land Rover came to an abrupt halt in its own cloud of dust. We eased ourselves out, gasping as much from exertion as relief. There was also an embarrassing sense of anticlimax: away in the distance, the test site was still quiet, marked now by only a few plumes of dark smoke.

Major Biddle massaged a bruised forearm while I grappled with the camera I'd brought to capture for posterity the image of the exploding stack. I used the Land Rover's bonnet as a makeshift tripod, focused on the distant smoke, and waited. Five ... ten ... fifteen minutes passed. My arms ached from holding the camera. Then the stack exploded with a bright flash and a loud and deep rumble. The echoes went on for a very long time. Major Biddle turned to me and grinned: 'Bet you didn't need a flashbulb for that one.'

The village had no name that I was aware of. The road I'd taken out of Benghazi soon gave way to a track which would have tested a goat, never mind a Land Rover. I pulled in behind an old German army truck whose condition matched the surroundings. It was barely conceivable that anyone could still be living here; the ragtag huddle of white breeze-block buildings looked as though they were falling apart in a kind of slow-motion earthquake. In amongst the dereliction, dogs barked.

Amal was in his early twenties and brimming with enthusiasm. He wore a white shirt and dark trousers and, for some unfathomable reason, a red polka-dot scarf tied loosely around the neck. In clear but fitful English, he introduced himself as Operations Manager of the centre of the breakdowns. For this was the place where Libyan workers dismantled all manner of munitions, sending the scrap metal to merchants and the explosive to Italy, where it was turned into fertilizer. (I was to remember this years later, when dealing with IRA bomb-makers who turned fertilizer into explosive. By that time, too, there were parts of Belfast which looked no better than this.)

Amal was recently promoted, the previous manager having been

killed in an ammunition accident together with several of the
workers. Gazing around at the buildings, I wondered if accidents
were routine here. Amal was grateful that the British army expert
had come to the centre of the breakdowns to give his good advice.
Safety procedures had all been improved, and it was hoped the
British expert would be impressed by what he saw and advise on
how to make things even better.

And so the inspection tour began. By rights it should have
finished less than five minutes later, but when you're the British
army expert you can't just head for the hills at the first sign of
danger. We ducked low through a misshapen doorway and entered
the first of the workshops. Ammunition, of every type and in every
conceivable condition, was stacked haphazardly in various corners
or piled up on benches where the dismantlers worked. It was
obvious that much of the stuff had come from sunken ammunition
barges lying just off the Libyan coast. The bodies of the shells
were well-nigh rusted away; great crops of multi-coloured crystals
had formed where the fuzes used to be.

I would have blown the whole lot up without touching it but
Amal's men had other ideas: they were happily levering shell from
cartridge cases and then pouring out the sodden propellant to dry
in the sun. God alone knew what Captain Scott would have thought
of it, back in Walsrode.

Amal beamed at me. 'You have some thoughts about this?'

I stared dry-mouthed as another case was split apart. 'It's a bit
hard to know where to start,' I said. 'The thing is –'

'Good,' said Amal. 'Good. Wait till you see some more of the
operation.' He turned on his heel. I trudged after him into another
building. For a moment, as my eyes accustomed themselves to the
change from bright daylight to inner gloom, I thought with all the
clanging and banging that I'd arrived in a blacksmith's. But there
were only three workers sitting cross-legged on the floor using
steel chisels and hammers to take the bottoms out of German army
anti-tank mines.

As before, Amal's presence unfortunately seemed to galvanize everyone into ever more feverish activity. I took two steps forward and stopped to stare at the floor: it was probably three inches deep in explosive; TNT dust hung thickly on the air and began to settle on my clothes. One of the mine workers looked up. He was wearing a polka-dot scarf around his nose and mouth.

'You see?' Amal said. 'Precautions.'

I wanted to tell him that, as precautions go, this ranked with changing into a swimming costume before tying your feet to half a ton of concrete and jumping into the sea. But Amal was hunched down by his men, and I'd no wish to join him. The situation was aggravated by the fact that, though I didn't know if this was an official operation or a private-enterprise 'cottage industry', it was certainly licensed by the Libyan government, so a certain degree of diplomacy was called for.

I diplomatically retreated to the far end of the room, where mines waiting to be dealt with were piled up side by side. To take my mind off what was happening behind me, I removed a mine from one of the stacks and reminded myself of the details of its design and construction. It was a Tellermine 42, a useful high explosive munition which could blow the tracks off any tank unfortunate enough to drive over a position where it was hidden – downward pressure was all it took to initiate detonation. I contemplated the stacks of Tellermines. There were enough here to cripple an armoured division. The majority looked in good condition but they all appeared to have been recovered from minefields and I wondered how the Libyans had overcome the problem of removing the fuzes: there was more than one model of fuze and one of these incorporated a booby-trap mechanism. This fuze was known as the 'Ti Mi Z 43' – Teller Minen Zünder Type 43; once the pressure plate of a mine was screwed down on such a fuze it was impossible to unscrew it without the fuze firing. As there was no outward clue as to which fuze had been used, it had become normal practice to destroy recovered mines without attempting to remove the pressure plates.

Because Amal was still down there amidst the TNT and because I had some reason for being as far away as possible, I pantomimed an elaborate interest in the mine, going so far as to unscrew the pressure cap and stare into the empty fuze pocket – except it wasn't empty. A Ti Mi Z *42* (the non-booby-trapped fuze model) stared back.

I looked at the stacks again, rapidly counting them. They all appeared to contain around twenty mines, one atop the other. A Tellermine 42 weighed 12 pounds; the pressure required to fire it was between 250 and 400 pounds. If a fuzed Tellermine was at the bottom of a twenty-high stack, it would be under a weight of 240 pounds; if a fuzed mine was at the bottom of a twenty-two-high stack, then 264 pounds would be pressing down on it.

I called Amal and showed him the fuzed mine. This, I explained, pointing to the stack, is *not a good idea*. Fuzed mines should *not* be stacked this way.

Amal smiled reassuringly. 'Oh, you must not worry. This is all safe. We know, we have experience of these things.' He lowered his voice. 'In the past, there have been ... accidents. A man unscrews the cap and *boom!* it goes off. Now we remove the explosive *before* we remove the cap.'

Realization dawned then that things were even worse than I'd thought: Amal's men were actually chiselling out the bottoms of *fuzed* mines. I swallowed hard. The reasoning behind this unique method of breakdown was now clear: once the explosive had been removed, then the pressure caps could be safely unscrewed because even if a Ti Mi Z 43 was fitted, only a small detonator in the fuze would fire. But such reasoning was dangerously flawed: the way the Tellermines were being stored and handled, the odds against ever reaching the stage of fuze removal were terrifying.

I tried to explain this but Amal either didn't hear or didn't wish to listen. 'The mines are all the same,' he said. 'Remove the explosive then everything good.' He nodded towards the trio on the floor. 'You see?'

I saw. I nodded – and decided it was time to go.

Outside, moving briskly away with Amal still in step beside me, I summarized the situation for his benefit: the mines, the fuzes, the TNT, the corroded munitions, the propellant – every last rule in the book was being broken. I would put it all in my report but in the meantime they *had* to start taking some elementary precautions.

Amal nodded as though each new criticism amounted to yet another endorsement, although by the time we reached the Land Rover there was sadness in his expression, as if the brevity of my visit indicated that he'd failed as a host. As I clambered up into the driving seat he said: 'Has it not been interesting for you?'

I gazed down at him and tried to think of something diplomatic to say. 'Amal, there's only one word for it: unforgettable.'

I started up the engine and the Land Rover pitched and swayed off along the track. I glimpsed Amal in the mirror before the dust cloud obscured him. He was waving and smiling again.

Libya, in 1956, was still classed by the World Bank as one of the world's poorest countries. The fourth largest country in Africa, it had been successively invaded by Egyptians, Greeks, Arabs and Turks. From 1912 to 1943 it had been held by Italy. Over ninety-five per cent of the land was desert or semi-desert, the two main populated areas extending inland from the Mediterranean coast. To the north-west lay Tripolitania, to the north-east, on the other side of the wide, sweeping Gulf of Sirte, Cyrenaica; both were under British military administration from 1943 until 1951, when Libya became an independent monarchy under King Idris.

I was sent to 624 Ordnance Depot, Benghazi, Cyrenaica, after the British withdrawal from the Canal Zone. The RAOC stores depot was housed in D'Aosta Barracks, originally built for the Italian army of occupation. There were two out-stations, a vehicle depot and an ammunition depot, this last a couple of miles from Benghazi. It held training stocks of munitions for the forces stationed in Cyrenaica together with reserve holdings for the much larger force that would be based here in the event of war.

In the early days of my tour of duty Libya seemed pro-British. As time went by, however, the rise of Arab nationalism, the emergence of Colonel Nasser and the effects of the Suez crisis changed things; when I left in 1958, terrorist bombings and riots were commonplace.

As before, my workload was heavy, particularly with clearance and disposal activity: Libya was littered with munitions left behind after the great battles of the Second World War, and tragedy struck at the most unlikely moments. During a visit to Tobruk the Queen of Libya and her entourage stopped to watch some Arab children playing a game similar to rounders. But when one of the boys finally hit the ball there was an explosion which killed him and seriously injured another child: the ball had actually been an Italian 'Red Devil' hand grenade. Horrified, the Queen asked King Idris to request British army help in clearing dangerous munitions from the Tobruk area, and thus I frequently found myself making the 220-mile journey east along the Alexandria road, past the groves and gardens of former Italian villas whose terraces looked out upon the deep blue of the Mediterranean.

Each week brought something new. Once I was called out by a member of the public in Tobruk, an unusual occurrence given that much of the Arab population continued to show a marked indifference to the threat posed by stray munitions. I couldn't work out if it was ignorance or fatalism or a combination of both; whatever the reason, the results were frequently lethal and sometimes downright bizarre.

Two incidents in particular demonstrated the scale of the problem. In the first, the Benghazi police had asked for assistance in the investigation of an explosion which had ripped through the Souk and left three dead and over a dozen injured. I couldn't at first identify the cause of the explosion from the physical evidence at the scene. Then I found an eye witness who told me that the blast occurred because an Arab welder, fed up with having his acetylene gas bottles stolen, had decided to weld his name-plate on to them.

The second incident was but the latest in a whole series: yet again we had discovered an Arab home with walls constructed with unfired shell. Normally the occupants refused to believe the shell was dangerous; they listened to us with great courtesy but ignored everything we had to say. On this last occasion, however, courtesy was notably absent – a reflection of the hostility increasingly permeating Libyan society, much of it stoked up by Egyptians who filled teaching positions at all levels of education. I was told that my presence at the house had less to do with matters of safety than with a plan by the filthy British to dispossess as many Arabs as possible.

On my way to Tobruk, I wondered what kind of reception I'd get this time. Following standard practice, I reported to the British army base in Tobruk and then set off for the incident location, expecting to find at least one or two of the local police on duty at the scene. Instead, a small crowd of Arabs was waiting by the ruins of what had once been a large villa, a merchant's home on the edge of Tobruk.

A series of holes had been cut into the floor. It wasn't necessary to look into them to divine their purpose: a nauseating stench signalled only too clearly that the locals were using this place as a public lavatory. One of the Arabs, a sort of official representative of the group, came forward. 'It's in there,' he said. 'In the big hole.'

He stepped between two of the smaller holes and beckoned me to follow. When we were at the biggest cavity of the lot he produced a torch and switched it on. The beam played on walls caked with faeces and veined with the tracks of dried urine, then shone downwards to a dark and semi-viscous mass alive with the black and bloated shapes of hundreds of crawling flies. The mass filled in the spaces between the walls of the hole and the cylindrical flanks of just about the biggest shell I'd ever seen.

'We thought the British army should be informed,' said the guide.

I didn't respond; with breath still held I continued to stare into the hole. Half hidden by the stinking filth, the shell had to be at least 15 inches in diameter. No weapon of this huge calibre had been used by land troops in the North African campaign so it must have come from a battleship on the Med. How it came to rest in the basement of the villa only God, or Allah, knew. I straightened up and stepped back, as though surveying the scene, aware of my companion's mocking scrutiny.

'You British know what to do. Or so they tell us.' His eyes gleamed with malice. 'You *can* deal with it ...?'

In situations like this you can either waste time trying to think of clever witticisms or you can get on with the work. I stepped past the Arab and went back to the Land Rover. Within a few minutes I'd made up a 5-pound satchel-charge and attached it to one end of a reel of detonating cord. I picked up the charge and the cord, grabbed a wooden pole, and returned to the villa.

The Arab continued to watch, his smile broadening in anticipation. I told him to get himself and his countrymen at least 400 yards away. The smile slowly faded and gave way to an expression of transparent uncertainty. He hesitated a moment longer, then walked over to the onlookers and began herding them to safety. At first they seemed reluctant to move, probably because there was still some last lingering hope that the filthy British soldier would get even filthier.

I secured the satchel to the end of the pole, then carefully pushed it down the hole, reeling out the detonating cord behind it. By jiggling the pole around I was able to drape the satchel-charge over the shoulders of the shell. I then knelt down, secured a detonator to the cord and a length of safety fuze, and lit the fuze. I knew I had about a minute to take cover.

Moving up-wind across a barren expanse of sun-baked mud which had once been the garden, I continued to distance myself from the villa's foundations. I stopped at the top of a slight rise and looked down on the unkempt landscape with its semi-derelict houses, burnt-out cars and patchwork of debris-strewn earth. Beyond, the roof lines of Tobruk shimmered in the sun, white domes and slender towers etched against the sea and the sky.

The shell exploded with a thunderous roar from all sides as the remains of the villa vanished in an eruption of smoke and dirt. Semi-vaporized by the detonation, hurled aloft by the blast, the contents of the holes became an ever-widening miasma, an enormous yellowish-brown stain that smeared itself across the sky. It hung in place for a few moments and then, caught by the breeze, moved slowly and remorselessly until, like some fine and delicate curtain, it began to come down on Tobruk.

My Arab friends emerged from cover and regrouped at the freshly sanitized scene. There seemed to be a lot of gesticulating and shouting but I was too far away to hear. It didn't matter anyway because they'd got nothing to complain about. The war had knocked the shit out of Tobruk. Now, thanks to the British army, it had all been put back.

And so the work continued: inspection of munitions, clearance and disposal activity, and investigation of accidents. Each week brought something new and something different, not least of them the case of the army vet who was shot by a horse.

Despite every effort to save it, the horse had reached the end of its days. The veterinarian assembled the humane killer, loaded the chamber, placed the plate against the appropriate part of the animal's skull, and hit the firing mechanism with the mallet. Unfortunately, the horse chose that moment to move its head. Mistargeted, the bullet glanced off at an oblique angle, ricocheted off a nearby ironwork column and wounded the vet in the thigh. The injury was relatively minor; I was glad the vet was OK and half-hoped the horse had survived, too, but the poor old thing was so stunned that the second attempt with the humane killer went as planned.

My accident investigation report made for curious reading. But it was as nought compared to the charge sheet in the Shebani affair.

Shebani was one of the civilian workers at the ammunition depot, a cheerful, elderly and bald Arab who spent most of his time tending the depot vegetable garden.

In his youth, Shebani had been digging a well when, several metres down, he found his progress blocked by a large rock. He called up for a pick and his brother obliged by dropping it on to his head. Shebani survived but still bore the scar, a circular indentation about half an inch across and half an inch deep.

On the morning I encountered him in the vegetable garden, he was clearly upset and close to tears. He didn't want to talk, still less explain why the top of his head had a patch of dried mud on it. Eventually the story came out: he'd been explaining his scar to some of our ammunition storemen and one of them had found it so funny that he'd taken a sunflower seed, placed it in the indentation, and covered it with mud. Shebani had been threatened with a beating if he tried to stop the seed from growing.

I'd nothing against practical jokes but when the victim was a defenceless old man then the humour ceased to be funny. I tracked down the storeman, a soldier called McPherson, and charged him.

The hearing took place in the office of the Major commanding the Ordnance Depot. The accused was duly marched in by the Company Sergeant Major and I read out the charge.

Trying not to look at McPherson, the Major, his adjutant or the CSM, I heard myself saying that the accused was charged with conduct prejudicial to the order and maintenance of military discipline in that he did on the day in question take a sunflower seed and insert it into the cranial indentation of a civilian employee, namely –

'Pardon?' The Major stared blankly at me.

'That, er, contrary to section five, subsection three of the regulations appertaining to –'

'The accused inserted a . . . sunflower seed?' The Major seemed to be having difficulty following all this. 'In a *what* indentation?'

'Cranial, sir.'

'A chap's *head*?'

'Yes, sir.'

The Major looked at his adjutant then back to me again. 'You mean we're employing a civilian with a hole in his head?'

'It's a sort of scar, sir. Caused by a pickaxe.'

The Major's eyes widened still more. 'McPherson hit him with a *pickaxe*?'

'No, sir. It was the man's brother.'

'Why? Were they having a fight?'

'It was an accident, sir. Some years ago.'

The Major exhaled noisily. 'That's a relief anyway.' He paused, shook his head in the manner of one wrestling with an ever mounting sense of disbelief. 'Well. Carry on.'

'The accused made threats of bodily harm if the sunflower seed was removed before the germination process had been concluded and –'

The Major had pulled from his pocket a handkerchief that now almost covered his face. Loud choking and gurgling noises issued from behind the handkerchief. Eventually he removed it and, with tears streaming down his face, ordered the CSM to remove McPherson from the room. As soon as the door closed, both he and the adjutant doubled up with laughter.

The hearing resumed some time later. Despite the earlier hilarity, the Major understood the potential seriousness of McPherson's actions, considering his threats of violence at such a politically sensitive time. McPherson was therefore reprimanded and confined to barracks for several weeks. It was a good way of discouraging him from any further attempts at gardening.

In the mean time terrorist attacks were increasing and, if the injury wasn't too bad, the insult certainly was: the majority of the explosives and ancillaries used seemed to have come from 9 BAD, now seized by the Egyptians. The bombs were simple things, usually consisting of a one pound block of Tetryl/TNT set off by a detonator fired by a Switch Delay Number 9.

That they didn't cause too much damage to our installations was due in part to the terrorists' frequent mismanagement. An attack on a fuel tank farm resulted in the holing of two structures but nothing else because the terrorists had targeted tanks containing diesel, which is very difficult to ignite. Three attempts to blow up the ammunition depot also failed. On each occasion a bomb was thrown over the perimeter fence from a passing car: the first tangled in the wire mesh, the second completely missed the storage site and the third hit a tree and fell harmlessly to earth because the bomber forgot to light the fuze.

An attack on the British Forces Broadcasting Compound also went badly awry. The compound was protected by guard dogs chained by individual ten-foot slip chains secured to a series of steel bars set just above ground level, an arrangement which allowed them to guard a predetermined area of the frontage. The bomber fed them some doped meat, then retreated to wait for the drug to take effect.

In his absence, however, a handler checked the zone and found that his dogs were semi-comatose. Anxious for their health, he took them away and chained up their replacements. The bomber returned and the wide-awake dogs duly dealt with not only him but also his bomb, as I found when I came to deal with it a short time later.

To provide a respite from official duties and the goings-on around us, the Ordnance Depot decided to stage an athletics meeting. Challenges were issued to the RAF base at El Adam and the Infantry Regiment at Beda. In the spirit of good Public Relations, the Libyan army was also invited to enter a team. To our surprise they accepted.

The field was neither Olympic nor sylvan, but it was level and had enough parched grass to make track events feasible. As the day neared, the event began to take on a carnival aspect; it was, after all, summertime and a rapidly widening assortment of organizers and volunteers seemed determined to make this the biggest thing that had happened in Libya for quite a while. The event committee included representatives from all the British units as well as the splendid ladies of the Women's Royal Voluntary Service, (WRVS).

The committee lacked for nothing in the way of ambition or imagination: a substantial £150 prize fund was created for the competitors, special free beer vouchers were ordered from the Printing & Stationery Unit, and a variety of side shows, stalls and specialty events were devised by the WRVS. A redoubtable matriarch called Mrs Ethne Powers took responsibility for the Donkey Derby, the highlight of what was intended to be a memorable and fun-filled day.

Bearing in mind the need to involve the Libyans as much as possible, it was proposed that they be given the job of buying the prizes. In 1958 £150 was probably worth what £1,500 is today; with that kind of money to play with, and their contacts with local shop-keepers, the Libyans, we thought, would be able to come up with some pretty remarkable prizes.

The great day dawned. I won the 100 yards, the 220 yards and the javelin, and was formally presented with a four-inch-high wooden camel, a small empty leather purse, and a bag of boiled sweets.

I thought about tracking down Captain Ellison to tell him about the prizes but by this time other things were beginning to crop up. Someone had fed the donkeys with an aphrodisiac – reputed to be freshly baked yeast bread – with the result that they were not so much in the mood for a derby as an orgy. Eeeh-awing all over the place, they had erections which dragged in the dust. Being of good English middle-class stock, the WRVS ladies were unfazed by the sight of rampant donkeys.

Walking back from the track, I chanced upon Mrs Powers as she whacked a donkey's penis with a stick.

In an effort to help I said: 'Excuse me, but I don't think that's going to do any good.'

Mrs Powers glared at me with a haughtiness which suggested that dealing with one prick was bad enough without another turning up to offer advice.

'I suppose,' she said, 'you speak from experience?'

I left her with her stick and grinning donkey for what was supposed to be the relative calm of the NAAFI, where I could exchange my voucher for a free pint of beer. But the NAAFI was in uproar: half of Libya seemed to be trying to get to the bar. The free beer vouchers had been intended solely for the use of event participants and helpers, but someone had taken advantage of the Printing & Stationery Unit's lax security to re-run the printing plate on one of the machines. As a result, thousands of the vouchers were now in circulation. That the NAAFI wasn't yet dry was due only to the fact that the beer had to cross the bar in glasses; with so many full glasses in so many hands the flow was temporarily staunched. Later that night it did run out, thanks partly to the efforts of enterprising soldiers who turned a bath in one of the barracks blocks into a storage tank and worked in relays to fill it, glass by glass.

Before I left Libya I saw some important new arrivals: survey crews from international oil companies in search of black gold. Ordinarily, civilian operations of this kind would not have involved me. But as the crews were encountering serious problems with uncleared desert battlefields and uncharted minefields, one of the companies sought my assistance. With the Commanding Officer's permission, I took local leave and spent three weeks with Oasis Exploration, a company set up by a multi-national outfit for the purpose of identifying Libyan oil reserves.

To do the actual sweeping I used twenty or so locals equipped with mine-detectors; they would identify and mark a suspect location for me to clear later. The range of munitions recovered was extensive; their general condition was very good, as I discovered for myself.

The tank was an Italian M40, a sun-bleached relic of war that shimmered amidst the desert sands. It had been hit by an armour-piercing round which had penetrated the hull then ricocheted around the interior, smashing everything it touched. The bodies of the crew had been removed but bone fragments remained in the debris together with at least one badly damaged shell. I didn't consider it wise to clamber about inside, still less to attempt the removal of the remaining ammunition. The safest solution was to burn the thing out.

I told my clearance crew to keep well back as I siphoned diesel from the tank and added a couple of gallons from our own petrol reserve. After dousing the interior, I laid a long train, set fire to it, then got back into one of the survey Land Rovers and joined the rest of the crew on a rocky hillock about 400 yards distant.

We brewed up some tea and watched the smoke rising from the tank. The fire seemed to have taken very rapidly; the pops and bangs issuing from its interior meant that the burn-out was going well. But then came a different bang, much louder than anything before, and a shell suddenly whirred overhead and vanished into the desert behind us.

It took a few moments to get over the shock and work out what had happened. The explanation, though incredible, was also simple: the main 47mm gun on the tank must have been loaded at the moment she was hit. The shell, which had lain in the chamber ever since, had cooked-off in the heat of my fire. Fourteen years after loading and aiming, the objective of a long-dead gunner had finally been accomplished.

On the eve of my departure from Benghazi Oasis offered me a permanent job. The attractions were many, not least the money: I had already been paid the enormous sum of £90 a week for my three-week stint with the survey team. Yet the uncertainties seemed to outweigh the advantages: as Oasis pointed out, if oil was found within the specified exploration period, then I had a secure and highly paid future before me. But if oil wasn't found, then Oasis, which existed only as a Libyan exploration arm, would close down;

those who worked for it would have no claim on the parent company.

I had made a lot of friends in the seismic crews so I asked them what, in their professional opinion, were the chances of finding oil. The answer was honest but discouraging: nothing had so far come to light that looked even interesting, never mind promising. Working for Oasis might be fun and well-paid, but it was still a gamble.

I turned down the job offer and said farewell to my friends. A few months later the first oil gushed out of the Libyan desert. It presaged the birth of an industry which would, in a remarkably short time, bring in $1,000 million per year and transform an impoverished country into the richest in Africa.

4

The Growth of Terrorism

====

When I arrived back in Britain in 1958 it seemed a very different place to the increasingly violent landscape of Libya and Egypt. It was not as well-ordered as in times past – but it was still a land where standards prevailed. Mugging was what people did when they needed to cram themselves with facts. Terrorism was something to do with foreigners in Palestine, Kenya, Cyprus or Aden. A bomber was either something on a fly-past through the sky above your head, or a cartoon figure dressed in black, not someone likely to crawl out from under your car. You could tell from what you read in the papers and heard in the pubs that the threshold of belief was universally higher; in England people did not go around making, placing, or throwing bombs.

Things were soon to change; a change that occurred almost imperceptibly but one which would bring about an irrevocable shift in the life and outlook of society.

I was working at Headquarters Ammunition Organization RAOC, Feltham, Middlesex, a place with army-wide responsibility for all technical matters relating to the storage, inspection, maintenance, disposal and proof of ammunition. It gathered in data and produced information and very soon I realized that I'd become a paper warrior.

There were, however, compensations; after a short spell in tented accommodation in Benghazi, Daphne and I were now in a comfortable little semi-detached not far from HQ. Our daughter Vivienne had been born in October 1953, but I'd seen far less of her than I would have wished. Even when we were together in Libya, Vivienne hadn't coped too well with the heat and so she and Daphne had continued to spend time away with Daphne's parents. In February 1960 our second child, Timothy, arrived and our family was complete.

I had been promoted to Staff Sergeant while in Libya. The rank lacked the resonance of the title given me by civilian staff at Benghazi: *Hadji Gamfous*, the first word meaning one who has been to Mecca, the second meaning hedgehog, thus 'Hedgehog who has been on a pilgrimage'. Thanks to my spiky crew-cut, the hedgehog aspect was easily explained; the pilgrim element less so. I had never been to Mecca and my forays into the desert had always had more to do with war than worship.

As time went by it became obvious that Feltham was not going to suit the Pilgrim Hedgehog; though the work was interesting, it was theory rather than practice. Still, the company was good: the avuncular Sam Birt, last seen in Bad Oeynhausen, was now at Feltham, as were three NCOs of kindred spirit: Ken Howorth, Roger Goad, and John Sheldrake. We worked out of the same office and shared the same interest in sport: Ken, a blunt but engaging Yorkshireman who had been in Tripoli while I was in Benghazi, was an excellent cricketer, Roger was a keen golfer and John a crack shot in small arms competitions. The camaraderie was strong and enduring.

Between 1961 and 1964 I returned to Germany, this time with No. 1 Ammunition Inspection Unit, Herford, BAOR. Even though Britain had changed when I returned in 1964, there was still little hint of a darkening sky. The Swinging Sixties were under way, their early innocent momentum fuelled by the sound of the Beatles, the sight of the mini-skirt and the smell of new money. Britain in general and London in particular were in the glare of the centre-stage spotlight, a position desired by all performers even though it blinds them to what might be going on in the wings.

I became senior instructor at the Army Apprentice College, Chepstow, in the department responsible for the training of ammunition technicians. It was, as ever, a British military world with British military preoccupations where skills were taught and learned and traditional codes of discipline and conformity maintained. As such it mirrored many of the civilian institutes of education, for the protest era was still in its infancy and the dawn of British urban violence not yet a glimmer.

At Chepstow, as elsewhere in the country, the significance of events far beyond Europe passed almost unnoticed; the headlines of August 1964 referred to summer heat and summer fun while the foreign news rated only a few lines: 2 August – US DESTROYER ATTACKED BY NORTH VIETNAM TORPEDO BOATS; 5 August – PRESIDENT JOHNSON ORDERS THE FIRST AIR STRIKES ON NORTH VIETNAM. The world was changing in the small print but few recognized it.

My first bombers on British soil were dangerous madmen who needed locking up. The appellation 'guerrilla' or 'terrorist' seemed inappropriate to their activities: Welsh nationalism was then more of an eccentricity than an emergency. Unfortunately, the perspective of the doer and the done by are very different; my new problem was the extremists' old cause, and an apparently bizarre aberration was noted by a shadowy few for later emulation.

I had gone to a quiet classroom in rural Gloucestershire to teach others the art and craft of the ammunition technician. It was not exactly dull but, equally, it was not exactly exciting. I was not to know that I had inadvertently gone to the one place in England where terrorists would strike.

The call came through from the army base at Hereford. The

problem, it was explained to me, was Welsh extremism. There was a feeling in Wales that it had for too long been under the yoke of the English and that now was the time for a change. None of this was news because the issue had long been chronicled by the British Press. It didn't amount to much more than the defacing of road signs. I still couldn't see what it had to do with me.

But then I was told that extremists had taken up the moderates' cause, and had decided to blow up the new road crossing over the River Severn, then in the course of construction. One of the world's longest suspension bridges, it was to most people a welcome link between England and South Wales. To the extremists, however, it signified the breaching of a natural barrier which could only lead to further anglicization.

Bomb threats against the Severn Bridge came within Hereford's area of responsibility; part of the Ammunition Inspectorate was actually based there. Unfortunately though, Hereford was a two-hour drive from the bridge; Chepstow was almost underneath it.

So on several occasions I found myself back on EOD (Explosive Ordnance Disposal) work, this time high above the River Severn. That every bomb turned out to be a hoax was of little comfort: when you're grappling with vertigo 300 feet above a raging river and the wind is trying to lift you from a perilous perch, there's no joy in discovering that the suspect box actually contains a couple of candles and a bloody alarm clock.

The EOD operatives tasked to deal with the situation referred to the extremists as the 'Viet Taff', but we knew they were dangerous. They knew exactly what they were doing: the hoax calls disrupted and endangered lives, and the few bombs that actually did go off caused terror in the streets. But public opinion did not call them terrorists, though that is what they were, because terrorism didn't happen in Britain. Besides, eyes were turned towards London where 1964's images of Carnaby Street and the King's Road had inexplicably been replaced by visions of anti-war protesters in violent running battles with the Metropolitan Police.

And so 1966 dawned and the Welsh extremist campaign continued. To many it was still just a joke. On 5 March 1966 the Irish Republican Army blew up Nelson's Pillar in the centre of Dublin. To many, that was just a joke as well.

I left Gloucestershire the following year for the Ammunition Repair Methods Development Unit at Command Ammunition Depot, Bramley. It was a return to fondly remembered territory as well as an opportunity to satisfy my interest in both explosives and engineering, for the unit was responsible for the design, development and testing of tools for repairing, proving and destroying ammunition and explosives as well as the design and development of EOD and CMD (Conventional Munitions Disposal) equipment.

Time passed quickly here, time spent in practical work on practical issues, with collective efforts that ranged from the sophisticated to the Heath Robinson, though all were underpinned with the same qualities of ingenuity and enthusiasm. As in 1950, so in 1967: Bramley was a place for learning and benefiting from others' expertise and experience, a military world facing new challenges.

But change was continuing outside. On 5 June 1967 the Six-Day War broke out in the Middle East. On 26 October anti-Vietnam war demonstrations erupted in Washington and London. Bloody war and violent protest were becoming the staple ingredients of newspapers and television alike. What had once seemed unthinkable in democratic societies were now increasingly commonplace: on 10 May 1968 Paris erupted in street warfare between students and police; on 5 October Londonderry burned itself into the headlines with the biggest civil disturbance yet seen in the province; on 27 October London was brought to a standstill by yet another anti-Vietnam war demonstration. The old battlefields had gone; the biggest war could now be fought inside the smallest street.

On 21 April 1969 troops were sent to Northern Ireland to protect key installations against the threat of terrorism. Five years earlier,

the very notion of UK soldiers being actively deployed on UK
soil would have been unthinkable.

That same year, 1969, I left Bramley for No. 1 Ammunition
Inspection and Disposal Unit (AIDU) in Hounslow. I was now a
senior ammunition technician with the rank of WO1 Conductor.
(The first meant Warrant Office First Class, the second was a
distinction dating far back into history, when the monarch would
require the provinces to supply cannon and other munitions for
war; the safe passage of these to the Royal Armouries was ensured
by his Conductors of Ordnance.)

No. 1 Ammunition Inspection and Disposal Unit was responsible
for all ammunition matters outside service ammunition depots in
the south of England; its duties included inspection of ammunition
and ammunition storage sites, ammunition proofing, accident
investigation, demolitions, EOD and CMD.

Work was not confined to military locations, for reminders of
the Second World War were still being unearthed on construction
sites in and around the capital. Members of the public – including
ex-Servicemen who should have known better – were still showing
a frightening lack of awareness of the dangers of wartime souvenirs: the shell that Grandfather kept as a trophy could and sometimes did spell the death of a grandchild.

The public tends to have a stereotyped image of what a bomb
looks like: a big, black or iron-grey metal object, often with fins,
and the word 'bomb' or some other identifying mark printed on the
side. The stereotype was perpetuated by *Danger: UXB*, a television
series shown a few years ago which starred Anthony Andrews as
a bomb disposal man. The image may be correct for aircraft bombs
but, in my experience, few bombs fall into this category. In fact, my
duties fell into two distinct areas: CMD (Conventional Munitions
Disposal) and IEDD (Improvised Explosive Device Disposal).

Conventional munitions such as grenades, anti-aircraft shells,
mortar bombs and aircraft bombs, are mass-produced to a known
design or pattern. You can look them up in a book and discover

the fuze mechanism, the amount of explosive and the hazards involved in their disposal.

With an IED you can't know any of this until *after* you have defuzed it. IEDs do not conform to any set pattern; if you gave a hundred people the same basic components to make an IED, they would construct a hundred different bombs.

Since every IED is different, there can be no prescribed render-safe procedure. Today X-ray machines can reveal some of the mysteries of the bomb's interior but you can still never be sure that you, or the X-ray, haven't missed something until *after* you have dealt with it.

Conventional munitions are seldom designed to kill the person who is trying to defuze them. Nor are they usually fitted with time fuzes so it does not matter how long your approach takes – if it has been happily lying there for fifty years, it is not likely to explode the very moment you walk up to it. On the other hand, IEDs very often have both these ploys: time fuzes and a variety of anti-handlers or booby-trap mechanisms.

I would not wish to denigrate CMD – after all, I spent half my career working with conventional munitions – but the challenge of the IEDD provides a greater sense of achievement, as well as the reward of knowing that you have helped to save lives or, in some cases, to convict the terrorists who planted the bomb. And, of course, the 'buzz' is better – the more dangerous the situation, the faster the adrenalin flows.

We were not the only agency to be operating in the London area: the Metropolitan Police Explosives Office was also active. Originally set up in response to an epidemic of safe-blowing (often by ex-National Servicemen using their military skills to personal advantage), the work of the Explosives Office had expanded from the early days when one of its biggest headaches was caused by incompetent burglars who shoved explosive into a safe's lock only for the stuff to fall uselessly inside.

No. 1 AIDU worked with the Metropolitan Police and the Met's

Explosives Office as and when required; as a result, Hounslow increasingly found itself dealing with incidents of criminal intent. On 11 December 1969 I responded to such a call. We made it from Hounslow to the Greek Embassy at a speed that is only attainable when you have blue flashing lights and a very loud two-tone horn. Bill Banfield, one of the staff sergeants at the Unit, was driving; the Austin 1800 saloon positively rocketed into the West End.

A senior police officer was waiting for me at the cordon, fifty metres from the embassy. I'd already had the details in the original call to Hounslow but it was wise to go through it again: not only could messages get garbled; during my journey the situation could easily have changed. When dealing with bombs of any kind you always moved at two different rates: high speed to the scene, and circumspectly thereafter.

'Looks like a live one,' said the officer. He nodded towards the embassy building, a bright oasis that spilled its light on to the deserted expanse of street. 'They were holding a reception and dance. Security checked the bag of a young man as he came in. They found two bombs.'

'What makes them think they're bombs?'

'There's wires sticking out all over the place and some sort of timing mechanism.' A wry smile. 'Dancing shoes they aren't.'

The bombs had been taken outside and placed in a dustbin prior to the evacuation of the building. Those who had come in search of entertainment had now found drama. I moved off down the side of the embassy. The background noise would have diminished anyway as mute expectancy replaced speculation, but this time the effect was all the more marked because of the sense of sudden isolation.

For the first time I was conscious of the loneliness of the long walk to the bomb, the journey an operator makes from the cordon to a bomb or suspect device. Though the distance is usually only about 150 yards, it can seem a *very* long walk indeed . . .

Nowadays, it begins with the donning of protective clothing,

Above: The Gurney family, photographed at Netheravon, Wiltshire, 1948. L to R: Peter, Edwin, Cecelia, Maureen, John and Diane.

Right: Peter with a 'blind' artillery shell retrieved from Larkhill Ranges, Wiltshire, 1946. Only later did he discover what a dangerous practice this was.

Above: Badajos Barracks, Aldershot – Peter's home during basic training, 1950.

Below: Peter and friend 'playing' soldiers, 1954.

Opposite Above: Bomb found in the Greek Embassy, London, on 11 December 1969 and defuzed by Peter.

Opposite Below: Staff Sergeant-Major Peter Gurney receiving a commendation for defuzing above bomb.

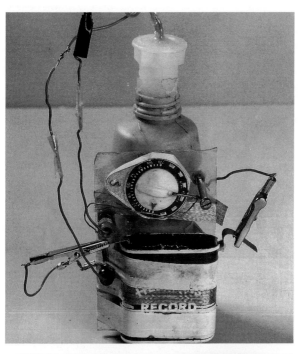

Opposite and Above: Sequence of three photographs displaying the effects of 12 oz of plastic high explosive detonating inside a Mini.

Right: Damage to a building near the Old Bailey car bomb, 8 March 1973.

Above: Car bomb outside the British Forces Broadcasting Service in Westminster. After defuzing the bomb, Peter removes 120 pounds of high explosive from beneath the rear seat squab.

Left: Peter in The Bungalow after receiving the MBE for Gallantry for defuzing two of the car bombs on 8 March 1973.

Right: A typical parcel bomb and its contents, after being defuzed.

Below: X-ray of above bomb, clearly showing two batteries, microswitch, wristwatch and detonator. The grey shadow at the bottom of the X-ray is 4 oz of high explosive.

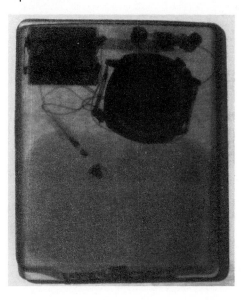

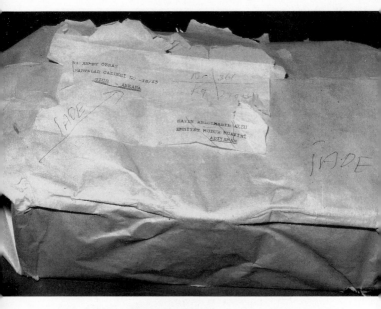

Wrapper from the parcel bomb
defuzed by Peter in Ankara,
Turkey, 1978. 'IADE' is the Turkish
acronym for 'Return to Sender'.

unavailable in 1969. There is a specially designed bomb jacket and
helmet with a combined weight of 22 pounds as well as a full bomb
suit and helmet which, at 52 pounds, is even more awkward and
restrictive.

The bomb helmet is probably the most important item of an
operator's protective clothing: it's one of those curious facts that
although the head represents around 14 per cent of body volume,
86 per cent of fatal injuries to bomb men are to the head. The visor
allows a forward view only; worse, when helmet, collar and bomb
jacket are all in place the weight is such as to prevent free movement of the head, so that tunnel vision results. In most situations
this is more an irritant than an impediment, but in others – for
example, where an operator has to negotiate a flight of steps –
great care has to be taken not to stumble or fall.

Inevitably, the weakest part of the helmet is the visor. Though
made of ⅜ of an inch thick Plexiglas, flying debris and bomb fragments can penetrate it. The bomb jacket is stronger, but it will stop
fragments and mitigate blast effects only up to a certain distance
from a bomb. After that – depending on the size and nature of the
device – there is no protection: the explosion will either maim or
kill you.

The closing of the helmet's visor is like the shutting of a door
on the familiar, everyday world. One moment you are there, at the
cordon, aware of the sounds and sights all around, the next you're
in an altogether different environment, a place where you can only
see straight ahead, and can only hear muffled noises from the world
beyond. The sense of isolation is acute. Like the underwater diver,
the loudest noise is your own respiration.

And so you begin the long walk. As you draw nearer to the
bomb or suspect device, thoughts begin to churn: every step brings
with it a new set of possibilities and considerations.

You find yourself calculating the effects of an explosion, subcon-
sciously mapping out imaginary boundary lines between zones of
relative safety, medium risk, high risk and probable fatality. But

the zones are pure guesswork, because unless you're certain of the size of the bomb, everything is speculative. In truth, you can never know the precise nature of the threat until you are on top of the bomb – at which point there's no sense in bothering anyway; if it goes off then you'll be dead within milliseconds.

With each step you inwardly compute such factors as probable poundage, environmental conditions, weather and distance from the bomb. As each invisible boundary line passes underfoot, you find yourself thinking about degree of body damage, about survivability; 100 yards, 75 yards, 50 yards . . . as the distance diminishes between you and the bomb so the likelihood of multiple injury increases.

In many ways, this is the worst time: to be close enough to a bomb to be maimed but too far away to be killed is the most deeply-rooted horror of all. You know what a bomb can do, how its blast can blind and deafen and tear away human limbs. To me, death is infinitely preferable to being stretchered away to hospital there to awaken in a permanent darkness knowing only that I will never walk, hear or see again. Far better to be at the bomb when it explodes, to exit this life quickly, cleanly.

But these are not the only thoughts which clamour in the silence and the isolation. Even whilst one part of your mind is calmly and dispassionately undertaking risk assessment, another part is calculating and re-calculating angle of approach, endeavouring to map out the safest line of attack. You know what is going through *your* mind – but what was in the mind of the bomb-maker and the bomber? Is all as it seems, or does a secret trap await?

All the time the gap is narrowing, with every step another zone is navigated, another invisible boundary line is crossed.

Finally, you are there and it is as if a whole section of circuitry shuts down. It is too late to speculate. Now there is only the bomb, and every last thought process is directed to it. Two options exist: either you will beat the bomb, or it will beat you.

You stop, compose yourself, steady your breathing. Taking

stock of the bomb's size, shape, location and possible intended target, you gather all the information the bomb will yield up without touching it. You make the decision on your line of attack . . .

The devices were side by side on top of the rubbish in the half-filled dustbin outside the Greek Embassy. I switched on my torch to illuminate the dustbin's interior.

If they weren't bombs then they were certainly fair imitations: what seemed to be home-made explosive was connected by a tangle of wires to a detonator and some kind of timer, a type I hadn't seen before: small, circular, made from moulded plastic and capable of fitting easily into a pocket or the palm of one's hand. The fact that nothing had happened when embassy security moved the devices didn't mean things would stay that way if I did the same. Better to deal with them *in situ*; being hunched over a dustbin might be uncomfortable but it was infinitely preferable to being blown up.

I rechecked the external details of design and construction and worked out the most likely configuration of the circuitry. Gripping the torch between my teeth, I stooped down over the dustbin and set to work with Stanley knife and wire-cutters.

Somebody once said that the first cut is always the deepest. A bomb disposal operative could also have added that the first cut is sometimes the last. In 1969, before the advent of portable X-ray machines and remote-controlled mini-robots, equipment was elementary: hardware was a pair of hands, knife, and cutters; software, a brain. Not only did the brain have to command the body's motor functions, it also had to think its way into the mind of a stranger – the bomb-maker.

Was that person skilled or amateurish? Was the bomb as simple as it looked or more complex? Alternatively, was an apparent complexity merely a way of causing confusion and delay?

You had to look, and think, and think again because what was at your fingertips was as much an expression of a stranger's personality as an expression of that stranger's purpose. It was warped, certainly; but just how warped? And just how cunning? All of which meant you couldn't go cutting the nearest wire without thinking everything through: get it right, and the device would soon be rendered safe; get it wrong, and there would be no second chance to contend with the likeliest cause – the collapsing circuit.

With such a circuit, current is fed from the battery to a relay – an electromagnetically operated switch. If you cut the wire that provides power to the electromagnet, the magnet will cease to function. The instant that happens, the magnetic field will collapse, and this causes the relay to close. With the relay in the closed position, the current will now flow directly to the detonator, where it is converted into heat, causing the small explosive charge in the detonator to ignite and then detonate. The shock wave from the detonator will blast into the main explosive charge, causing instant decomposition. This will set up a shock wave that will flash through at supersonic speed, exciting the individual molecules of the explosive which then release super-hot gases and immense energy.

Sometimes a bomb will have more than one collapsing circuit (the IRA was later to come up with a device which actually had seven). Sometimes the wire itself will cause problems: cutting a co-axial or a twin lay-flat can lead to a shorting-out which also initiates detonation. Even when a wire is single strand it can still be deadly: if you don't take care to keep it well out of the way after cutting, it can drop down and short out against the casing, thus allowing the current to pass through to the detonator (on at least one occasion a bomb disposal man was killed by inadvertent mishandling of a cut wire).

Whatever the cause, collapsing circuit or shorting out, the resulting sequence of events occurs in milliseconds and is entirely unstoppable.

Hunkered down over the dustbin, my jaw and mouth throbbing from the strain of holding the torch, I gripped the wire between the cutters and squeezed. A few moments later I heard the ticking of the timer.

The significance of the Greek Embassy bombing only became apparent when the bomber was brought to trial. Guilt wasn't in doubt, nor purpose: the attack was politically motivated. There was, however, a dispute about what had happened. The defence said that the bomber had not set the devices and so they were quite harmless; the prosecution said that the bomber *had* set them because the explosives disposal operative at the scene had heard a ticking noise.

Defence Counsel confronted me in the witness box and handed over one of the unfamiliar-looking timers.

'Mr Gurney. You said in your earlier evidence that you'd heard a ticking sound. Presumably it was emanating from this timer?'

'Yes, sir. I heard it soon after I'd cut the wire.'

'But the defendant says he never set the timer. So how d'you account for that?'

'The timer definitely made a noise. It was a . . . metallic sound. A high-speed ticking.'

'I see.' Counsel paused. 'The timer – if you hold it in front of you, would you say it's about as far from your ears as it was on that night?'

'More or less.'

'So you can hear it ticking now?'

I strained to listen. Finally: 'No, sir.'

Counsel smiled. 'I can assure you, Mr Gurney, the timer is definitely set. And yet you say you cannot hear anything.' Another pause. 'This Courtroom, is it as quiet as the location which you were at on the eleventh of December 1969?'

'I would think so, sir.'

'You would think so.' Counsel paused again. 'It's no noisier here than it was outside the embassy yet you can't hear any . . . ticking sound.'

'No, sir.'

'Mr Gurney. The fact is, this type of timer does not make a clearly audible ticking when it is set. More to the point, it did not and could not have made any noise *at all* on the night in question ... because the defendant had not set it.' A brief though eloquent pause. 'Whatever you might have heard, Mr Gurney, it was certainly *not* the ticking of a timer.'

The silence ran on between us. Eventually, and with the utmost politeness, Counsel reached for the exhibit. 'May I?'

I leaned forwards and handed it to him. At that same instant it burst into life – a high-speed ticking ... noisy, metallic. 'That's what I heard!' It was an effort to keep still. 'That's the noise I heard.' The sound continued. Across the Courtroom, the jury heard it too.

This timer was to become increasingly popular with motorists. It served as a reminder: you parked your vehicle at a metered bay, set the timer according to how many hours or minutes you'd bought on the parking meter, then went off about your business. Safely in your pocket, it would alert you to the fact that time had run out by emitting a noisy and metallic high-speed ticking.

I had not seen this unit before the night of 11 December 1969 and therefore hadn't known that, had I not cut the wire only a few moments before, the ticking would have been instantly followed by an explosion. The timer's name was to become very familiar to me and many others because the Memo-Park Timer and the IRA were later inseparable.

In 1970 Hounslow dealt with 3,200 CMD calls, ranging from a single item to 15 tons. Our involvement with matters criminal rather than civil increased as a reflection of the increase in the politics of violence. IED calls mounted, thanks to the activities of Black September, the Palestinian terrorists, and the anarchist Angry Brigade.

The Metropolitan Police had decided to build an impressive new police station at Paddington Green, and huge hoardings testifying to its construction were erected around the building site. You couldn't miss what was going on – nor could the Angry Brigade.

At around midday on 22 May 1970 a site worker almost tripped over a small newspaper-wrapped package. Assuming that one of his colleagues had misplaced his lunchtime sandwiches, he picked up the package, shouted to his friend, and tossed the package across to him. His mate unwrapped the newspaper and found a bomb.

I was called to the scene and briefed by a Met liaison officer who asked if I could preserve as much as possible of the device for forensic evidence. 'If you can sort of stun it first,' said the liaison man, 'we'll be able to go in close. Get some shots. Afterwards you can do whatever's necessary.'

I examined the bomb. It had already unwittingly been thrown around; after that kind of treatment it was likely to be more delicate than ever. I knew I'd be able to disconnect part of the circuit and render the timer inoperative, but that would only make the device safe enough to be photographed. As I emphasized to everyone at the scene, a 'stunned' bomb is still a bomb: it must not be touched until I'd made it totally safe.

It was a good day to be outdoors. Sunlight sparkled on concrete and steel and warmed the soft brown earth. I finished the preliminary work, straightened up and motioned the Met photographer to join me. He was carrying a large-format camera, accessories and a tripod.

'I'll take some overhead shots,' he said. 'That all right?'

'So long as you don't touch it, yes.'

He extended the tripod's legs; slowly, carefully, I positioned it in such a way that the anchor plate was directly above the bomb. He attached the camera to the plate, satisfied himself that the tripod was secure, inverted the pan/tilt anchor, and centred the viewfinder on the bomb. He took two photographs and then paused to adjust the lens before resuming. 'Right,' he said, frowning slightly. 'That about does it from that angle.'

I glanced at him, then back to the bomb. At this stage of the proceedings my gaze had to stay locked on the device. 'Anything wrong?' I asked him.

'It's the light. I don't want to throw the thing into shadow by standing in the wrong place. And I don't want lens flare, either. If you look where the sun is you'll see that –'

But I was still looking at the bomb and the overhead camera and the tripod – and the tripod legs that had suddenly assumed a life of their own. Slowly, progressively, they were splaying outwards under the heavy weight of the camera. Slowly, progressively, the camera was dropping down on to the bomb.

I launched myself forwards in a kind of sprawling dive, grabbed at the camera and tripod and pulled them away. I finished up flat out on the earth, a couple of yards from the bomb.

The photographer stared open-mouthed, then moved to my side. His face bore an expression of enormous relief. 'Thank God you caught it in time,' he said, reaching for his camera. 'These Hasselblads cost a bloody *fortune*.'

Around this time we were experimenting with a new aid to EOD work: a portable X-ray machine. Though it was still wise to think yourself into the bomber's mind, having something to hand which could actually look inside a device was going to make life a lot safer.

We had a Swedish-made ScanRay unit on test. It weighed only marginally less than a hospital's entire X-ray suite. X-rays taken by the unit were developed separately, which meant we resembled a sort of travelling film crew going out on location.

We were always anxious to try out the unit in as many different conditions and on as many objects as possible, so when a call came in from a museum in Colchester we loaded up and headed off to Essex. This time, it was not munitions but mummy trouble.

The mummy was 2,000 years old and still wearing its original outfit. The curator had decided that the mummy was due for the equivalent of a 2,000-year oil change. Its wrappings were beginning to come apart and, as mummies went, it was no longer in first-class burial chamber condition. Could we, enquired the curator, X-ray it to see if the embalmed body was wearing any jewellery? Well, of course, we could; the nice thing about mummies was that though they could go off, they didn't do so with a loud bang. Deterioration was preferable any day to detonation.

We moved in close with the ScanRay and X-rayed the mummy from every angle, then took the exposed film plates to our hi-tech mobile laboratory (the back of a truck) and laboriously developed each picture. They were impressive: from head to foot every detail was clear. Of jewellery, though, there was no sign.

The following week another EOD call came in. A blind three-inch mortar had been unearthed in a town-centre location; traffic was stacking up and if the situation couldn't be speedily resolved there'd be chaos.

I made it to the scene as quickly as possible, taking the ScanRay equipment and fresh film plates for further trials: the machine would hopefully give me a pretty good idea of the condition and content of the bomb – drill filling or high explosive – and that would determine whether or not I could safely move it to a less inconvenient area for disposal.

It was a day when everything went well. Not only did the ScanRay function as intended, a nearby hospital was able to process the plates far more quickly than I could: it seemed I'd hardly arrived before the X-ray staff had finished the job and had the plates pinned up on a back-lit display for inspection.

'Pretty good,' said the radiographer, as he walked slowly along, studying each image in turn. I thought so too as I trailed after him, inspecting the results of my handiwork. Then, 'What on earth is this?'

He was staring at the final shot, brow furrowing with incomprehension. 'I don't understand . . .'

Nor did I. The X-ray showed the mortar and something else, a strange mixture of substance and shadow, rigid white structures of varying thickness coming down then radiating out around and above the bomb's upper casing. Bits of curling whiteness were also dotted about the image.

The radiographer leaned closer to the wall. He spoke very slowly. 'Unless I'm very much mistaken,' he said, 'that's a metatarsal.' Disbelief gave a rising inflection to his voice. He jabbed at the image with his finger as though to better confirm its existence. 'A metatarsal . . .'

Oh Gawd, I thought. The last time I'd seen an image like this, I'd been poring over it in the company of the museum curator at Colchester. This last X-ray must have been accidentally omitted when we processed the batch. As a result, the plate had gone back into stock, become mixed up with the new film, brought to the EOD scene – and then been inadvertently used by me.

Instead of taking a single picture, I'd actually managed a most artistic double exposure of a fairly modern mortar and a very ancient mummy's foot.

I turned to the radiographer. He was staring at me with the kind of look which medical people reserve for the dangerously irresponsible or downright deranged.

'You don't mean to tell me,' he said, 'that when this X-ray was taken you were actually *standing* on the bomb?'

I hesitated. This was going to require an awful lot of explaining.

X-ray machines were to prove essential in the fight against terrorism. A few airports, but by no means all, had X-ray scanners in 1970; only later were they to become as essential as a runway. But they were not (and are still not) a hundred per cent effective against terror in the skies. On 21 February 1970 two aeroplanes were targets for bombs: an Austrian Airlines jet which managed to land safely despite extensive damage, and a Swissair jet which blew up high above Switzerland with the loss of everyone on board. It was obvious that some new and very elaborate precautions were going to be needed.

The bombs had been placed in parcels for international Air Mail. The targeting was entirely indiscriminate: there was no way the bomber could have known which aircraft would be operating the route because all scheduled carriers convey Air Mail.

As a device it had been simple enough: batteries and explosive wired to a detonator via an altitude-sensitive barometric switch. The higher an aircraft flies, the lower the pressure falls. A barometric switch detects the decrease in pressure and, when it declines to a point predetermined by the bomber, allows current to flow between battery and detonator to initiate detonation and explosion of the main charge. Obviously, the key to the bomb's operation was the functioning of the barometric switch. If conditions similar to those of a high-flying aircraft could be replicated, then international package post could be screened before going into an aircraft's hold. The only problem was, how do you duplicate the conditions of a jet at 30,000 feet?

At Hounslow we were asked if we could devise a method of simulating the depressurization effect; Air Mail packages carried by BEA and BOAC could then be handled very much more quickly. In the wake of the 21 February explosions, all such mail was being manually checked before loading.

We had worked out a theoretical solution to the depressurization problem; now it was time to test it out on the edges of Heathrow Airport. We transported a large galvanized iron watertank to our little patch of noisy desolation; the structure (around 7′ × 3′ × 3′) was big enough to house three or four mailbags at a time. Next we wrapped the tank in a preposterously voluminous 'Driclad' heavy-duty plastic bag. It looked bizarre but, when closed, the bag ensured a completely airtight covering. We then installed a valve which ran through from the bag's outer skin and into the tank. When coupled up to a vacuum pump, the valve allowed us to evacuate air from the tank's reinforced interior, reducing internal pressure to that in the cargo hold of an aircraft flying at cruising height.

Soon fed up with our windswept test site, we commandeered a Post Office workmen's hut, tapped a power source from a nearby aircraft landing light to provide electricity and heat, came to an amicable arrangement with airline catering firms who thereafter regularly stopped by to drop off free meals, and finally set two large pots of geraniums outside our front door.

Teething problems with the chamber were to be expected: sometimes the valve didn't operate as smoothly as it should have; on other occasions the airtight seal didn't hold. Nevertheless, in a very short time we got the depressurization chamber up and running. Its performance quickly became dependably consistent. For a cost of less than £200 we had built a depressurization chamber that worked first time, every time.

Today airports throughout the world have depressurization chambers which embody the same principle we applied at Heathrow. They can cost up to £500,000.

Aircraft were not the only form of transport threatened. The nation's favourite ship, the *QE2*, had been the subject of an unusual extortion attempt: someone had rung Cunard to say they'd placed a bomb on board and unless a very large sum of money was paid then Cunard's prized possession would very soon find itself at rest alongside the *Titanic*.

Cunard alerted the police. The police alerted the army. The army went through its records of bomb disposal officers to discover how many had parachute experience. Only one could be found. He was duly flown out across the Atlantic to parachute into the sea near the *QE2*. No bomb was found and no bomb went off. The extortion attempt had been a hoax; when the deadline passed, nothing was heard from the caller again.

When word subsequently came through that the army needed experienced explosives officers to volunteer for parachute-training, I responded immediately. It would be marvellous: everyone knew it took at least a month to train a parachutist and in our case it might even be longer. I could get into shape again after too much sitting around inside offices and Land Rovers.

I reported to RAF Abingdon, Oxfordshire. The base was extensive and swathed in vast expanses of green grass. There had to be a running track somewhere around; I felt the springy turf underfoot and breathed in the fresh country air.

Six EOD officers had reported for parachute-training, including two from Hounslow: myself and Alan Brahmer, an athletically built staff sergeant with a sharp sense of humour. We made our way to the classroom for the induction session.

My only slight worry was that I couldn't swim. It was, if you thought about it, a disadvantage, but no more so than my fear of heights. Surely within the time available it would be perfectly possible for the RAF to take a non-swimmer who suffered from vertigo and turn him into an expert parachutist ready at a moment's notice to drop into the ocean anywhere in the world.

We listened to a briefing by the Senior Parachute Instructor. 'You are being trained for waterborne landing. You are being trained for this because the army does not want you disappearing down a ship's funnel, never to be seen again.

'The procedure is very simple . . .' And he gave us a long, complicated demonstration of how to deal with a parachute. At the end he paused and smiled understandingly. 'I know. It seems a lot to take in. But I assure you, by tomorrow afternoon all this will be second nature.'

Tomorrow afternoon? I would probably have swallowed hard if my mouth hadn't suddenly turned so dry. Far from having a couple of months before making our first parachute jump, we were not even going to have a couple of days.

We went to the training area and stared up at a replica rear hull that had been created to simulate the aircraft jump-off point. Another instructor began checking off our personal details as we arrived.

'I think you should know something,' I told him. 'I can't swim.'

'That's all right.' He smiled. 'If your chute doesn't open we'll be able to put it down to death by drowning.'

Long hours of practice now followed: how to fall, how to go through the mechanics of the process, left hand here and right hand there, and this strap and that strap, and arms across, arms up, legs bent, legs straight and, finally, 'The moment you exit the aircraft you open your mouth and shout *"Geronimo!"* as loud as you can. Altogether now: *Geronimo!*

'*Geronimo!*'

The echoes dinned around the replica hull. The instructor seemed pleased. 'That's right, "Geronimo". Never forget it.'

One by one we stepped into the wide maw of the hull and dropped down on to the surface below. From the interior, the last sight we had of our colleagues was their fingertips gripping the lip and the last sound their ringing war-cry: *'Geronimo!'*

Alan Brahmer preceded me, vanishing from sight yet somehow contriving to leave his fingertips behind. Eventually his head slowly reappeared as he hauled himself back up. 'Excuse me, Sergeant,' he said in his usual well-modulated tones. 'What was the name of that fucking Indian again?'

With less than a day's practical training behind us, we were thundering over the Channel in the company of a squad of Special Boat Service personnel. The white face of the one sitting next to me prompted me to ask him if he was training too. He told me he'd done around 300 jumps. Just think of Geronimo, I told myself. Everything will be all right.

I fell like a stone, then like a bird, and finally like a butterfly. The red haze cleared from my eyes soon after the racketing and battering of the aircraft had faded; when I looked around, it was already nearly a mile away. The sea, the coastline, spread out far below; after the pre-jump tension, the utter serenity was blissful. I'd never felt so free before.

'Geronimo,' I said. But this time it was only an awed whisper.

I landed in the English Channel and came up to find my canopy still floating on top of me. I struggled free of the thing and the spare chute that had somehow become tangled around my legs and then bobbed up and down in my Mae West, gasping for breath.

The Gemini rescue craft soon reached me. The Marines told me

I'd come out of the water like some strange sort of penguin, actually walking the last twenty feet to the Gemini. I didn't care. The excitement, the elation and the overwhelming sense of satisfaction meant that all I wanted to do was to get back up there and do it all over again.

It was not to be. I never made another jump. I returned to Hounslow and subsequently went on an EOD update course at Bramley, where I encountered Lieutenant Colonel Alan Yardley, then Chief Ammunition Technical Officer, UK Ammunition Inspectorate. We had met in the past; now we talked about the way the bombers were bringing terror to Northern Ireland. I said I couldn't understand why the army wasn't sending out WO 1s; after all, we were the most experienced in the RAOC. I would be more than happy to go.

I didn't get to finish the update course. Two days later I was in Belfast. It was August 1972 and Northern Ireland was in flames.

5

Belfast

===

They had left the car in a narrow alleyway off the Crumlin Road – three youths in jeans and windcheaters with a handgun apiece. The car had stopped in the mouth of the alley, hemmed in by buildings on either side. The driver and front passenger got out and waited with guns poised while the third youth manoeuvred around in the back. It took him barely half a minute to finish whatever he was doing, and then he also clambered out of the car. One of the escorts then shouted at the bystanders: 'There's a booby-trap bomb in this car. Youse got five minutes to get the fuck out.'

The call came through to the Ops Room at Girdwood Park where I was based: suspected car bomb, Crumlin Road west, emergency services and ground troops attending. I was on day one of a seventy-two-hour roster: operational for the first twenty-four hours, on standby for overflow work in the next twenty-four, on stand down for the third.

This latest outbreak of 'the Troubles' had first erupted in 1969 and 1970. In that two-year period only 167 explosions occurred in the province; 1971 had witnessed 1,022 explosions involving 9,600 pounds, and 274 finds totalling 1,040 pounds of explosive, with

508 bombs containing 2,700 pounds being defuzed. By the end of 1972 1,339 explosions would have occurred, involving 48,500 pounds of explosive, with 561 hoax calls, 1,259 false alarms and 621 finds of explosives totalling 26,900 pounds. The number of bombs defuzed stayed roughly the same as 1971 (515), but the bombs were on average nearly *eight times larger* and involved a total of 20,500 pounds of explosive.

Faced with such a fast deteriorating situation it was obvious to the army that Northern Ireland could no longer be a standard three-year RAOC posting. As a result they devised a system whereby suitably qualified ammunition officers would be selected to carry out four-month-long emergency tours. They were initially drawn from UK postings and, as I'd noted, hadn't included anyone of Warrant Officer Class 1 rank.

The senior Explosives Ordnance Disposal officer in Northern Ireland was a colonel with a major as second-in-command and support staff all based at HQ, Lisburn. Operational duties were assigned to three RAOC detachments – one in Londonderry, one in Crossmaglen, and the third in Belfast. Each consisted of a captain and four ammunition technical officers (in Northern Ireland both commissioned and non-commissioned ammunition technicians are known as Ammunition Technical Officers – ATOs) plus signalmen and drivers. Also attached to each section were four infantry soldiers to serve as the duty Ammunition Technical Officer's bodyguard.

I had been in Belfast just over six weeks when the Crumlin Road call came in. There was now an average of twelve incidents a day, some of them hoaxes, most of them not. The IRA had split between the old-guard 'Official' wing and the new-style 'Provisionals'.

Bombs which had been crude to begin with were now as ambitious as anything fashioned by terrorists elsewhere. The bomb-makers now knew how to create home-made explosive, how to install timers and how to arm them with relative safety. In their early endeavours devices had been carried to the scene in a dangerously unstable state, but they'd rapidly learned to make bombs which could be safely transported, armed at the target, then triggered by electric circuitry linked to variable-delay timers. IEDs (Improvised Explosive Devices) they may have been, but they were complex and sophisticated, improvised only in the sense that they had not come from licensed munitions manufacturers.

Now it looked as though I had yet another IED to deal with. I left Ops and headed outside to where the Saracen was waiting in the yard. It roared along, pitching on corners, bucketing over the road surface, every vibration travelling from its six wheels through the huge armoured frame.

The police had set up a cordon 200 yards from the alley in each direction; ground troops and other RUC officers were at each end and appliances from Belfast City Fire Brigade waited, engines ticking over. Flagged by the waiting ground troops, the Saracen double-parked near the railings and I clambered out.

A breeze funnelled between the buildings – an angular row of two-storey terraces, a warehouse, and petrol station on the right, a twenties or thirties apartment block on the left. Leaves and scraps of paper stirred in the gutters. Other than that, stillness; and yet beyond the cordons, beyond the army Land Rovers and police vehicles, everything was normal: distant figures thronged the urban landscape, cars and trucks and buses wove in and out of the traffic flow. At the cordons bystanders pressed forwards, clusters forming and regrouping, voices beginning to carry on the air. The clearest voices were the highest voices. They belonged to the smallest onlookers, girls and boys aged eight or nine, ragtag kids with pale faces and hands thrust deep into the pockets of their jeans.

The senior army officer at the scene briefed me: suspect vehicle – Riley Elf, colour blue; IED believed to be in rear interior; location – the alleyway between the petrol filling station and the paint store.

Some thought had obviously gone into setting up this incident:

a paint store, a petrol station, an IED in between – this was typical
Provo planning. Women carriers often hid between their legs
incendiaries housed in small audio cassette boxes. They would take
the device into a store and set it down out of sight, hidden away
amongst paper, paint, plastics or upholstery. When the thing went
off, fire would consume everything. If it was timed to ignite late at
night, then a £2 incendiary could do £2 million worth of damage.

This particular bomb could be an elaborate hoax designed to
disrupt rather than destroy. Given the eye-witness statements,
though, it sounded more like the genuine article, a bomb hidden
in a cardboard box on the back seat of the car. I hoped it was the
only one. It took only one pound of high explosive to blow a car
to pieces, but the IRA had been known to use up to 500 times
that amount: a small bomb was placed in plain sight and the bulk of
the explosive hidden away inside luggage and inside compartments.
The explosive could be commercial or home-made: this bomb could
well feature the widely used Co-op recipe (a filling of nitrobenzine
and sodium chlorate, so called because the bombers first tested out
the efficacy of the mix on a Belfast Co-op store). As for the timer,
the IRA had given a five-minute warning, but that didn't mean
anything and ten minutes had elapsed anyway. Whatever was in
the car could go up now or at any time.

Thoughts flickered through my mind in the space of a few
seconds – no more than that, because if you are an EOD operator
you don't go to a scene to stand and muse. All you know is what
you see and what you have been told – and you don't necessarily
trust that.

You do not entertain any preconceptions because what is happening to you now has never happened before. What you are going
to do now you may very well never have done before. Every kind
of possibility exists as you move out from safety and begin the
long walk.

The car was obviously going to have to come out. The stubby
boot and thin gleam of chromed bumper almost filled the alleyway.

Depending upon the size and nature of the device, an explosion here could at best smash a lot of glass, at worst bring down the wall of the paint store and spark a conflagration. The petrol station was actually less volatile; its storage tanks were under ground.

I moved in closer, constantly shifting my approach. As usual, the problem was how best to get to the IED location. Walk along the pavement, close in to the walls, and if a device goes off the suction effect of the blast will whip out the windows and create a lacerating blizzard from myriad shards of glass. Walk along the gutter, away from walls and windows, and the blast wave will lift roof tiles like straws in the wind and send them arrowing down. Alternatively, move out into the road and the risk of death is even higher: not only is there a probability of being struck by the bomb's fragmenting casing and anything else hurtled outwards by the blast; there's also a chance that someone near by may have you in his sights and –

'SNIPER!'

Even as the sound fully registered – a distant *thwack!* of something striking stone or brick – the warning shout cut through the air. I hit the ground, rolled, heard it again, *thwack!* – another bullet, not close though, perhaps not even intended for me.

I scrambled away from the junction. The troops had obviously sourced the fire to the flats. Whether they would lift the sniper was another matter: by the time a soldier had raced up God knows how many flights of steps the shootist would have either escaped along a backstairs route or simply slipped into his own apartment.

I got back to the Saracen, pulse calming, steadying. There would be 10,628 shooting incidents in Northern Ireland that year and in at least four of them I was a primary or secondary target. It wasn't something I shrugged off or forgot but equally it wasn't something that left me quaking with shock, unable to continue. After all, everybody got shot at in Belfast: policemen, ambulancemen, firemen, soldiers, children. (Soon after I arrived in Belfast, a corporal whose section was attending my IED incident advised: 'If you hear me shout, "Take cover", sir, please don't ask where. You'll be talking to yourself.')

The ground troops seemed to have the situation under control. Back at the Saracen Dave Cook, my number two, helped me to rig up what is the best life-saver ever developed for use in bomb disposal activity. About three feet high and constructed from light-weight tin plate and aluminium, the 'Wheelbarrow' trod where angels and sensible EOD operators dare not. It looked like a refugee from a low-budget sci-fi film, a rudimentary wheeled robot powered by a couple of 12-volt batteries and driven by an electric motor which whirred discreetly as it trundled to its target. Yet it was highly sophisticated and capable of undertaking a variety of tasks.

There were rival designs, but they had proved horrendous, especially the 'Skate'. This had 2-inch wheels and 2-inch ground clearance. When you sent it along the road to a suspect vehicle it would suddenly veer into the gutter, its wheels banging impotently against the kerb until you came out of cover and retrieved it. Another was called the 'Dalek'. It weighed God alone knows how many kilograms and had a turn of speed that would have disgraced a snail. I had been encouraged to use both the Skate and the Dalek but found the best way to deal with the bloody things was to blow them up.

The Wheelbarrow was different. Invented by Peter Miller at the Military Vehicles Experimental Establishment at Chobham, the electrically powered machine originally had a rope-operated tiller but had been progressively refined. Soon there were electrically steered versions all operated via a remote control console linked to the unit by a length of command cable.

The inventor was as distinctive as his invention: you could ring Peter from Belfast and say the barrow didn't cope too well today, and somehow he'd wangle a flight out the next morning and solve the problem. It was the kind of behaviour which probably didn't suit the orthodox minds that ran MVEE because when Peter retired there was virtually no recognition of his work, nor has there been any since. His invention has saved many a life. He deserves far more acknowledgement than he has received.

Hunkered down by the side of the Saracen, Dave and I watched our Wheelbarrow whirr away. We'd rigged it with an automatic snap-on towing hook, the idea being to position the barrow by the car then trigger the spring-loaded release. After the hook with its towline had been clamped on to either the suspension or back axle, the barrow would be detached and moved clear. With the free end of the line secured to the Saracen, the car would be towed out backwards into the middle of the road. If the IED went off then, the resulting damage would be far less.

Navigating the barrow was now second nature to me. The control unit had fore and aft controls and a rotary knob which you turned to activate the secondary switchgear. The main thing was not to get the control cable fouled up in the wheels.

I edged the barrow along the left-hand pavement and then, at a point almost opposite the alley, swung it around the concrete column of a street lamp. Because of the Elf's position (the alley was at right angles to the road) there was no way of getting a direct pull. I then manoeuvred the barrow across to the Elf and triggered the spring release. There was a satisfying clang of metal on metal as the hook arm clamped on. I disengaged the barrow, using the fore and aft controls to move it clear.

We hooked the free end of the towline to the Saracen. The high thick-ridged wheels began to turn and the Elf slowly emerged, its wheels passing over the control cable that still snaked from me to the barrow. The youths had most likely left the handbrake on and the car in gear to frustrate such a manoeuvre, but when you've a 1-inch diameter nylon towline coupled to an 11-ton Saracen the outcome isn't in doubt. The Elf stopped safely in the middle of the road. I brought the barrow back to the Saracen; like an obedient retriever it waited, whirring.

The safest way of dealing with the IED was to send in the

barrow again, this time with a 'Candle', a 6-ounce charge of RDX/ Aluminium (cyclo-trimethylene-trinitramine mixed with aluminium to enhance the blast and burn effect. The principle was simple: when the temperature of a flame is increased then so is the temperature of the escaping gas; the greater the temperature, the greater the volume; the greater the volume, the greater the blast effect.) I took a Candle from the protective case and began to wire it up. The Candle would be attached to a boom on the barrow, just aft of the unit's automatic window-breaker. The barrow would then be manoeuvred alongside the car, the window-breaker aligned at a right angle to the glass, and the barrow driven slowly forwards until contact was made with the pane, whereupon the pressure caused the window-breaker to function. The barrow would be inched forwards again until the end of the boom was inside the car; at the press of a command switch, a signal would race down the cable, activate the boom release, and the Candle would then drop neatly on to the seat.

But a Candle isn't impact-sensitive; you don't just drop it to make it go off. In this instance the Candle's detonator would be attached to fifty yards of light twin-core cable held on a drum on the Wheelbarrow. After the Candle had been dropped, the barrow would be brought back towards the Saracen. As it travelled along the drum would turn and the detonator cable reel out behind it. As soon as the barrow was out of the major blast area, the firing circuit switch could be triggered to initiate detonation. The result, we hoped, would be to destroy within milliseconds the firing circuits of the IED and burn out its explosive.

I held the Candle under my left armpit, leaving both hands free to connect up the detonator leg wires. It looked smooth, waxy and quite innocuous. Yet within 8,000th of a second of detonation occurring, a Candle's blast wave will have smashed into an object a metre away with a force of over 400 kPa (kiloPascals) at a speed of over 700 yards per second.

Were you unfortunate enough to be next to it at the time, you'd

witness the sequence in all its spectacular detail: first the blue flash
of initial detonation, a few milliseconds in duration, then the impact
of the blast wave travelling outwards, fragments of casing spraying
in its wake. After that would come the secondary, orange flash, the
effect of air rushing back into the vacuum created by the blast
where it would mingle with the combustible gases and instantaneously catch fire.

I finished rigging the Candle to the barrow's carrier arm and
told Dave and the driver to get out of the way. I looked along the
street. The road was still empty, the pavements still deserted. I
flexed the command cable to remove some of the slack, picked up
the control box and knocked the switch to send the barrow out and
away from the Saracen. The motor whirred. The barrow juddered,
moved a few centimetres, then stopped. It just stood there, whirring
and vibrating. I worked out later what must have happened: the
Elf's wheels had actually scrubbed the command cable as the car
had been dragged from the alley; all nine conducting cores had
been stripped of insulation. All it had needed was for someone to
grab the cable and flex it, as I had done, and the cores would touch
each other and start arcing out as soon as the command circuit was
activated. This meant that the barrow was now able to work
through its full repertoire of actions without anyone touching the
control box.

The Candle dropped from the barrow's arm and lay still, less
than a yard away. A malfunction was the last thing I needed at a
time like this: there was an IED out there still waiting to be dealt
with. If the barrow was now going to start playing silly buggers
the whole operation would be delayed.

Along the command cable, unknown and unbidden, the arcing
continued to track across the conducting cores, making the barrow
shudder, triggering signals in high-speed sequence ... triggering
the firing circuit. I was still staring at the Candle when the blue
flash came.

The Candle had fallen to the ground in such a way that the main force of its blast went away from me. But there was still enough force to pepper my stomach with road gravel and to leave me bleeding from nose and ears; to lacerate my driver's face and to drive the fabric of Dave Cook's trousers into the flesh of his legs. There was enough explosive energy to hospitalize them both and stall the progress of the operation – at least, until I picked up another Candle, came out from behind the Saracen, went back to the car and tossed the Candle on to the back seat. The Candle blasted into the bomb hidden in the box on the car's back seat and destroyed it before it could do its job, then set the bomb's explosive on fire, and the car too.

I didn't stay to watch but went off to hospital to see how the others were and get myself checked out. My head had been ringing ever since the first Candle detonated but that hadn't mattered much at the time. Now the doctor peered in my ears, gave me some aspirin, and said I'd have trouble hearing properly as I grew older. Time proved him right.

Home was Girdwood Park Barracks, a sprawl of single-storey aluminium-sheet buildings alongside Crumlin Road Prison. They accommodated a Commando Group of Royal Marines and the RAOC unit consisting of a captain, myself and four other senior NCOs, all of us ammunition technical officers; the north part of the camp was dotted with brick buildings housing the Ulster Defence Regiment. Behind the high walls, the security fencing, weapons towers and searchlights, life pursued some small semblance of normality: a non-alcoholic bar, small shop and, thanks to the Army Catering Corps, cook-house food that was both considerable and well-nigh constant.

My first meal of the day would be cereal followed by a massive cooked breakfast and then toast plus enough tea to float the *Titanic*. Lunch would often be something like gammon steak with all the trimmings, dinner, a choice of roasts or steak. In between I'd stock up on banjos – sandwiches of egg or bacon. But I still lost weight:

no amount of food could compensate for the vast quantities of energy that all of us were burning, out there beyond the gates, in the tribal landscape of Belfast.

From the air, it was not an unattractive city, an ordered place of grey stone and slate overlooked by green rolling hills and threaded by the River Lagan. You would have thought yourself anywhere in Europe until you saw the façades of buildings waist-high in sandbags; the one-dimensional terraces with blackened roofless frontages; the burnt-out cars rusting away on rubbish-strewn wasteland; the barriers and fences and gable-end walls that glowered with murals and graffiti. You saw paintings of King William of Orange on his white charger, or the Red Hand of Ulster, and knew the Loyalists laid claim to the neighbourhood; paintings of men in anoraks and balaclavas and an outline of Ireland blocked in with solid green meant that you were on Republican turf.

Messages similarly betrayed the author's identity: NO SURRENDER! and IT IS BETTER TO DIE ON YOUR FEET THAN LIVE FOREVER ON YOUR KNEES were common. And sometimes you saw what happened when those charged with keeping the warring tribes apart finally had enough of the blood, the smoke and the shoddy stupid rhetoric and made a contribution uniquely their own: THOUGH I WALK THROUGH THE VALLEY OF THE SHADOW OF DEATH I FEAR NO EVIL BECAUSE I AM ONE MEAN BASTARD (1ST PARA).

You saw all this and checked your own private map, the tribal map that showed the middle-class Protestant population east of the Lagan, the Catholic areas across the river – New Lodge, Ardoyne and Unity above, Andersonstown, Turf Lodge, Ballymurphy, Springfield, Clonard and Lower Falls below, rent asunder by the sprawling Protestant enclaves of Shankhill, Springmartin and Glencairn.

Time for sightseeing, however, was limited. In a twenty-four hour operational shift you could be tasked to twelve separate jobs, some of them taking two or three hours apiece. You made it back

to the barracks and slept dreamlessly and briefly, then worked up
to twelve hours on the twenty-four-hour standby. In a forty-eight-
hour period you could be out for up to thirty-six hours and in that
time you learned never to wonder about anything.

The sign was on the wall of the control room the day I first
reported for duty: LAUGH AND LIVE. I might not have fully comprehended its meaning at that moment, but I learned to very soon
after. And the moral has stayed with me ever since.

It is, in fact, a saying familiar to all involved in the fight against
the bomber, a reminder that humour is your best friend as well as
your best weapon against the enemy.

It's often a black humour, but that is dictated as much by circumstance as individual predilection: when times are bad, as they often
are, and the demands of the job weigh heavy, the bad-taste joke is
a safety-valve through which pressure is released and frustrations
eased.

True, it can be cruel, but usually only in those cases where the
butt of the joke is infinitely more vicious. Which is why, for
instance, there's no need of apology for expressions such as 'own
goal' (a phrase commonly used when a bomber is killed or injured
by his or her bomb) or the wisecracks that spring forth after such
an incident ('if they ever get him to court, he won't have a leg to
stand on', or 'it isn't true he lost his balls because there's one in
the Bomb Squad office and another in the Kings Road', or 'that's
one bomber who's totally 'armless').

To an outsider, this kind of macabre humour may seem repellant
– as if we should show more concern for the victim in such circumstances. To be honest, the only concern I've ever felt is that the
bomber should've taken more of his kind with him.

But the humour is often directed inwards as well. For instance,
we all have our own particular fears about different types of bomb,
about certain features of their design or construction which we
especially dislike. Most operators tend to keep their private
thoughts to themselves, but in Northern Ireland one individual

became so voluble about his principal preoccupation that there was no option but to shut him up.

The time bomb was his favourite subject: what it was, what it meant, what had been required of him in the various situations when he'd been called upon to deal with one. The fund of stories and lectures seemed endless; we grew bored stiff listening to tales about timer mechanisms and the speed of the ticking and the nature of the timbre.

An opportunity to redress the situation was presented thanks to the mode of operation in Northern Ireland, where an operator is always accompanied at the scene by a number two, a colleague whose responsibilities include assisting the operator to don protective clothing and bomb helmet.

Once the helmet is on and the visor is in place, it can be difficult to hear what your colleague is saying, especially as he will be standing behind you (because the jacket fastens at the back). For that reason, the number two signals that his task is complete, and your task can begin, by tapping you on the helmet, at which point you then trudge off towards the device.

On this occasion, however, the number two did not tap the bomb helmet but instead affixed to it, with double-sided adhesive tape, an especially loud timer mechanism known as a 'Jock Clock'. The action occurred unbeknownst to the victim: as far as he was concerned, the usual signal had been given. Off he went – only to slow down after three paces and then stop. 'My God,' he said, 'You're not going to believe this, but I can hear the bloody thing ticking from here...'

A nail bomb is a simple tin – a beer or baked bean can – filled with explosive, packed with nails, and incorporating some kind of safety fuse. A crude grenade, the nail bomb is used for throwing at army patrols. However, because of the awkwardness of lighting the fuse (it can be difficult if you are nervous or a strong wind is blowing: you have to hold the match under the fuse's waterproof cover and as close as possible to its black powder train) it's no always obvious that the train has been ignited. The thrower must therefore decide within two or three seconds whether to hurl the missile on the assumption the fuse is lit or hang on to it on the assumption that it isn't.

This uncertainty led to many nail bombs being thrown with the fuse unlit, and soldiers got into the habit of picking the things up and bringing them back to us. The IRA soon learned of this through its network of spotters – the man on the street corner, the woman at the window, even the child leaning against a bicycle. So they took to leaving seemingly unlit nail bombs in places where soldiers would be likely to pick them up. A mercury tilt switch could be added to the device to ensure that it exploded as soon as it was moved. After the first death, the first maiming, all failed nail bombs were left where they were, to be dealt with by the EOD operators.

It was to just such an apparently harmless device that I was summoned one grey October afternoon. The drizzle had finally stopped and the slate roofs of red-brick terraces gleamed metallically under a low leaden sky. The terraced houses ran tight in against the boundary of an inner urban semi-industrial area; the bomb was in a corner formed by two brick walls at the edge of a match factory.

A crowd had gathered. You could tell by the looks on the faces and the taunts and the insults that you'd been deliberately drawn to a Republican area where too many reserved their sympathy for the terrorist and too few for the terrorized.

When I'd first arrived in Belfast I'd felt sorry for the Catholics, for people who had clearly been an oppressed minority, discriminated against by a Protestant élite which though it pledged allegiance to the British Crown was rather more loyal to its own self-interest. Like the newly arrived soldiers on their first street patrols, I'd thought these people might understand the simple facts of life. That *we* weren't the ones who were destroying their city. Blowing up their places of employment. Denying them a future.

Women would thrust their faces at a soldier's and scream and spit at point-blank range. Men with vacant expressions would look on, take another pull on a cigarette, then smile. As for the children, I'd already learnt what childhood means in some parts of Belfast: within a few days of arriving, I'd just finished dealing with a suspect device when a member of the crowd detached himself from the others and came towards me. He got to within two or three paces of me and then made to throw a large stone. But the stone didn't fly because the stone-thrower was only two years old, dressed in a romper suit and barely able to walk. He tottered on his little legs, almost fell with the effort of hefting the stone. One of the troops picked him up by his braces and carried him back to the crowd. They screamed at the soldier and fussed over the toddler.

And now I was being watched by another hostile crowd as I went forward to check out the nail bomb, inwardly noting that because the crowd was pressing forward, the odds were probably against a booby-trap: the onlookers wouldn't be that close if someone from the IRA hadn't already passed the word that the device was harmless. Even so, they were too close for comfort – twenty-five, maybe thirty yards away.

I knelt down to examine the device. A chunk of rock whistled past me and people yelled, applauded, screamed abuse; it was like trying to work in the presence of a manic Greek Chorus. I shouted to the troops to push the crowd further back, then turned back to deal with the device. Another missile was thrown by the crowd but I didn't see or hear it. Concentrating on the suspect device, I was oblivious to everything else until a soldier touched my arm and gesticulated at my clothes.

I had been wearing my bomb helmet and a combat jacket over my flak jacket. The outermost garment was smoking from the back, near my shoulders. I wrenched it off as well as the helmet, coughing at the sudden uprush of acrid fumes. The white smoke surged and steamed and I realized what had happened: as soon as I'd turned my back on the crowd, a bottle filled with battery acid had been thrown at me. It had hit the wall above my head and the acid had sprayed down over me. The paint peeled from my helmet and the fabric of my jacket disintegrated. It didn't pay to think what would have happened to unprotected flesh.

Another incident in Belfast, the bombing of the Nite Bite Snack Bar, saw me, as with the Candle, very lucky.

It was a popular city-centre haunt patronized by those who, like the majority of Belfast folk, were determined to ignore 'the Troubles'. Its presence was a reassurance to many that despite everything, life could still go on. The IRA decided to demonstrate otherwise.

The building next door to the Nite Bite was undergoing major renovation. The IRA went in and placed a 20-pound bomb against a concrete pillar and surrounded it on two sides with a mini-wall of house bricks. The bomb's blast could thus be channelled directly towards the Nite Bite Snack Bar and its unsuspecting customers.

I arrived after the bomb had gone off. The tunnel effect of the blast had done its job: people dead, people maimed, the unassuming little rendezvous reduced to a smoking pile of rubble and glass and fractured woodwork. When a 20-pound bomb is positioned with such precision and its explosive power directed in such a way, the outcome is a foregone conclusion. The ambulances wailed in the distance.

There was a possibility of a secondary device; I moved carefully through the wreckage. Not long before people had been enjoying a meal out. Now broken tables and chairs lay in tip-tilted confusion; smashed crockery crunched underfoot. Items of shredded clothing and purses and handbags were scattered everywhere. I made my way into the kitchen area, or what was left of it. A giant refrigerator had been blown over by the blast, the door wrenched back and the contents spilled out, most noticeably a huge pile of prime Irish pork sausages – enough to feed a small army.

The sausages looked good. Soon they would be trampled on

and scooped up and thrown away. I had a better idea: I would rescue some and we'd be able to add sausage banjos to our staple diet. I reached down and grabbed at the first sausage – and regained consciousness about thirty seconds later on the other side of the room.

The small portable tape recorder I used on jobs to make a contemporaneous record of what I saw and found and thought told it all. After the initial thud, the tape recorder ran on for a near silent half-minute and then played back the sounds of moaning and groaning as I came round.

I carefully hauled myself out of the debris and stood unsteadily, trying to clear my head. Then I went back to the sausages and carefully lifted them with a piece of wood. They were lying on top of a ruptured three-phase cable. A three-phase carries 440 volts – more than enough to kill. Why it didn't kill me I don't know.

The sequel to the Nite Bite Snack Bar bombing came three years ago when I had a full medical, including electrocardiograph. The doctor considered the ECG results then told me to sit down. He seemed to be having trouble forming his words.

'So?' I said. 'What's the matter?'

'Well, Peter, it's like this. You've had a heart attack.'

'Never.' I shook my head. 'I know what a heart attack is and I definitely haven't had one.'

A series of exhaustive hospital tests were arranged. They showed scarring of the cardiac tissue. The hospital consultant smiled regretfully. 'Sorry, Mr Gurney. There are all the signs of a heart attack – unless, that is, you've ever suffered a severe electric shock?'

I remembered then. 'I did get a shock, once.'

'How recently?'

'Seventeen years ago.'

'Must've been a major shock, then. What kind of work were you doing to come into contact with such a voltage?'

'You might not believe this,' I said, 'but it had a lot to do with sausage sandwiches.'

During my four-month tour of Northern Ireland I didn't make more than three or four off-duty excursions. In part this was due to the lassitude that struck after the nervous intensity of operations, but mainly it was due to the risk: the IRA would dearly have loved to wipe out every EOD officer in Northern Ireland.

Terrorist spotters would watch the camp to see which vehicles came out and then note the registration numbers of non-military vehicles. It meant we had to use nondescripts – cars which looked like average civilian vehicles – with false plates. At least there was no shortage: we worked our way through endless cars which had to be blown up because they either contained bombs or were thought to do so. We'd retrieve the plates, bring them back, and affix them to our nondescripts.

The theory didn't always work out in practice: one ammunition technical officer used a nondescript for a shopping trip and tagged it with plates from a car involved in an earlier incident. The only problem was, that car had been on the wanted list; before it could be taken off the list, a patrol spotted its plates on the nondescript and an EOD team was summoned. They promptly blew it up. When the ATO returned with his shopping he found his car reduced to a pile of burning wreckage and his colleagues standing around with the look of people satisfied by a job well done.

I was tasked to the scene not because of the first report of a body in a van but because of a second report which warned of a booby-trap. The van was a medium-sized commercial which had been stolen and finally located in a quiet neighbourhood, parked innocuously against the kerb. The RUC were waiting for me when I arrived. Like me, they knew the terrorists would booby-trap anything: a car, a culvert, a corpse.

Before I went forward the RUC detective said: 'I wouldn't dream of influencing the way you work, but if there's any chance of preserving as much of the body as possible for forensic purposes . . . ?'

I first checked the front of the van: nothing. I went round to the back. The rear door was partially open; I examined it carefully for signs of a booby-trap then clambered in. Boxes of meat were stacked along both sides of the van and against the far partition separating the load space from the driver's compartment. An island was formed by more boxes stacked side by side in the middle. Blood was splattered around the van interior. A man was lying on top of the central stack.

I moved cautiously towards him. He was lying face down, his hands tied behind his back with electrical flex. The ends of the flex had been pushed into his pockets. It could be a sign of a tidy mind or an indication of some kind of circuit. I checked him carefully, eventually determining that the flex didn't connect up to anything. If the body was booby-trapped, the bomb would have to be underneath him. The question was: where?

They'd made him lie down before killing him, forcing his face into a plastic tray half-filled with mince and shooting him through the back of the head. I reasoned that no terrorist would be stupid enough to position a bomb in any of the boxes underneath the mince tray and then shoot the victim from above. So if I cut a way through the boxes below the head I would have safe access to the rest of the stack.

I began with the box immediately beneath the mince tray, carefully cutting out one of its sides. This weakened the box and it collapsed. The mince tray tilted. And then the ticking started.

Tick, tick, tick. But nothing else. I waited a lifetime until it seemed that the device wasn't working. I could feel the inner tension beginning to ease, the paralysis of movement falling away like discarded shackles. I'd been resigned to dying – yet here I was, still hunched down next to a corpse in a meat van in old Belfast. And then I saw why.

The sound had not been made by a timer but by a single 9mm bullet rolling across the ridges of the plastic tray. The victim had been shot several times through the head; this round had passed clean through and dropped out.

It took me a long time to work carefully through the vehicle and its contents; the interior got hotter, the smell got worse and the buzzing of the flies grew noisier. There was no booby-trap.

I worked on conscious of what I'd *thought* was about to happen to me and, perhaps because of that, was more conscious than I might otherwise have been of what had actually happened to my companion. I wondered what he must have thought in the moments before his death. Perhaps he'd believed that his captors only intended to frighten him until they'd shoved his face into the tray of mince, and then he must have realized, in those few final seconds, that he was going to die.

Somehow that job summed up Northern Ireland for me, the viciousness, the grotesque brutality, the way the ordinary all too often hid the obscene. Anywhere else, a meat van parked against a kerb would be a sign of commonplace routine, you wouldn't look twice at such a vehicle. Unless you were in Belfast.

Cars rather than vans were the terrorist's preferred vehicle for a precisely targeted attack. We destroyed them because there was no point in risking a life merely to save a mass of rubber and metal.

It sounds simple, but when a car is burning up all manner of curiosities occur – the lights come on, the horn sounds, even the starter motor sometimes whirrs; finally the handbrake cable goes. That's why, if a car is parked on anything other than level ground, you first shoot out the kerbside tyres to stop it moving.

Unless there's a bomb or there's so little in the tank that it's filled more with petroleum gas than actual fuel, cars burn rather than explode. Only on celluloid does one see spectacular blasts of disintegrating metalwork — I know: I've tried shooting holes in petrol tanks. Even that only triggers fierce jets of flame.

Cars would occasionally be burned out even when they didn't contain bombs: sometimes you can't be absolutely certain of a vehicle's status until after it has been burned out. You can tell which is which by the performance of the fire: a blaze will dramatically intensify in both sound and colour when the explosive starts to burn, at which point it's time to get out of the way and head for safety.

For the people of Belfast this is often impossible. The city is a battlefield, and there are times when only fatalities are well documented; the injured are not news for long. One bomb blast in particular brought this home to me.

We make it to the scene at the same time as the emergency services. The route is congested with ambulances and fire engines and police vehicles. The reflections of blue lights track in rhythmic procession across the ground-floor windows of office blocks and stores; the sirens' yowl rises high above the centre of Belfast.

The Saracen shudders to a stop with the escort vehicles pulling in behind. An ambulance goes past and then another; their sirens cut off in falling cadence to be replaced by the staccato of feet running across hard paving, the noise of people shouting, the softer sound of sobbing. They're still bringing the casualties out.

We rarely get called to a scene when the ambulance crews are still working – they don't want us in their way and we don't want them or anyone else in ours. We either prevent incidents or we arrive when the scene is as clear and secure as circumstance allows.

This time though, things are different: what began as an alert has, in the course of our journey, turned into a reality. Someone is trying to explain things to me. I'm not immediately sure of the identity of the speaker because it's impossible to look away from the surreal scene. The large building of concrete and glass has a grassy apron in front of it that's increasingly turning to mud as more and more figures run across and the wheels of the ambulances churn up its perimeter. People are lying about on the grass as though it's high summer in the park instead of a weekday winter's afternoon in the city. They are obscured by coats and blankets and people clustering around them, people with dressings and bandages and soft voices and urgent hands.

The more I see, the more I absorb the battlefield conditions. Some of the wounded are propped up against the wall, others are standing with heads bowed; still more, far more, are down on the ground, on the lawn of an office block in Belfast.

There's a girl near by who has no one with her. I can tell she's young because even though she's lying down with back half-turned her dress has a youthful style.

Minutes seem to be ticking by and yet they're only seconds. Everything feels slowed down because of the sheer volume of information received by the ears and the eyes, because of the way the brain chases thoughts and sensations at speeds so fast that activity actually accelerates into a kind of blurred stillness.

The girl is trying to get up now, so I go to her. Her movements are very awkward; I think she must still be shaky from the explosion. I can see that her arms and legs appear to be OK. I'm sure that, with my assistance, she can get up, until I'm at her side and looking into her face.

There isn't any sound from her. There isn't, now, much sound from anywhere else. Sirens and shouts and sobs are muted. The distancing effect is taking hold.

I kneel beside her on the grass. She still wants to get up but I tell her it's not a good idea and she seems to accept that. Reassured, she lies back, resting against me. I hold her hand and say things to calm her but she has stopped struggling now. I don't think she knows where she is or what has happened to her or who I am. I know she can't see me because she can't see anything. She has no face. I cradle her to me and keep the words coming from somewhere. Just once she moves her head as though listening. Through the holes where her cheeks used to be her few remaining teeth clench together, then part.

I am reassuring her, I think, and calling for assistance. A medic arrives. Others are coming too and with them the return of sound, the return of wider vision; the world is no longer just two people on the grass in front of an office block.

The warning said there was a bomb in a car parked near the north end of the building, so an orderly evacuation was immediately organized. The building featured emergency fire escapes at both its north and south ends – stone or concrete steps which zigzagged down behind the huge ground-to-roof windows. A concrete balustrade was built to normal hand-holding height.

The women were brought from their offices to the south end of the building. They were still descending the emergency escape in an orderly crocodile when the bomb went off . . . at the south end.

The blast dissolved the vast expanse of glass and blew it inwards, into the people on the stairs. The shards travelled at incredible speed, slashing and stabbing and slitting and slicing. Because the concrete balustrade protected the women from feet to upper waist, the breast, shoulder and facial areas took the full force of the glass storm. Without the balustrade, many would have died instantaneously. Because of the balustrade, they were cut to ribbons instead. The blast did only superficial damage to the building. Repairs were needed to the external cladding and the windows but that was all.

The day after it happened, the news was about people being injured rather than people being killed, about a building that survived rather than a building that fell down. Because of this the media gave it less emphasis; newspapers do not sell on headlines like NONE DIE IN NORTHERN IRELAND BOMBING; BUILDING SLIGHTLY DAMAGED. Unless an explosion occurs in mainland Britain, and especially in London, UK national and regional Press and television will headline only those bombs which cause death and destruction, corpses and conflagration.

Of course people might die the day after the day after a bombing, but by then it is too late because the story has been heard before. To count in the headlines it is necessary to die before the deadline.

So I don't know what happened to those caught up in that bombing. I don't know if they all survived or if some of them died of their injuries in the days or weeks or months afterwards. I don't know what has become of the girl I held to me in the intervening twenty years. If she survived, she will have become one of the hundreds maimed and crippled by the IRA. Each incident inflicts different horrors on different victims, leaves a legacy of pain and disability that goes on long after the news has been forgotten.

Twenty years ago the IRA slightly damaged the exterior of an office block in Belfast, smashed some glass, and injured forty people. In the chronicle of IRA terrorism, it is very small beer indeed. Some who were there on that day still remember it: the ambulance crews, the doctors, the medics, the helpers, the police, the firemen, and the people like myself. Others who were there also remember it, but they have reasons more compelling than ours.

I left Northern Ireland at the end of 1972 with memories of bombs and killings and corpses and the sound of sirens. Though many of these memories blur together because of the similarity of context, some do not. One of them is all about a girl trying to get up from the grass.

6

The Bungalow

====

'Well,' said Geoffrey Biddle, 'Egypt it isn't, but it can still get pretty hot.'

My mind went back seventeen years to the explosive wave propagation test that had sent us sprinting across the sand to Geoffrey's jeep. Now, in February 1973, we were colleagues again, this time at the top of five flights of stairs in a building with no lift: Cannon Row Police Station. Outside, a cold drizzle fell; a gunmetal-grey Thames flowed sluggishly under Westminster Bridge.

I had come back from Northern Ireland in December and said goodbye to the army. After twenty-three years I needed a change. During my time at Hounslow I'd heard about the Met's Explosives Office: with only a desk job looming if I stayed in the army, it offered job satisfaction and an opportunity to display ingenuity, logic and independence unconstrained by army regulations. The Black September and Angry Brigade campaigns had shown London that the Improvised Explosive Device had arrived; the bomb-disposal man could now pit himself against bombs far more complex and challenging than those unearthed in Conventional Munitions Disposal work.

Geoffrey hadn't changed much over the years; he was still tall and ramrod straight with white hair, patrician features and clerical manner. He had been one of the founding members of the Met's Explosives Office, back in the days when safe-breaking had been all the rage. He had joined with Don Henderson, another ex-officer I'd known from my time in the army. Since then Ronnie Wilson and Andy Clarke had joined, so now there were five of us.

We were not policemen but civil servants, part of the Met's C7 support service. We were accommodated within the top floor of Cannon Row Police Station because it was close enough to the river crossing to facilitate south and north London operations and also because of its proximity to the seat of government.

In 1974 the powers that be decided we would be better placed in a home of our own – after all, being stuck on the fifth floor of a building without a lift wasn't ideal. We'd taken to waiting outside in the patrol cars during major alert periods: charging up and down five flights of stairs was not only tiring and time-consuming, it posed an unacceptable injury risk.

We were allocated an adjacent single-storey building which, imaginatively, became known as the Bungalow. It had originally been built as an Army Recruitment Office during the First World War. It took several months to get the accommodation into shape, during which time the Explosives Office was relocated on the ground floor of the police station.

By the time we moved into the Bungalow our numbers had swelled to eleven Expos. Amongst the new arrivals were two old friends: Ken Howorth, who joined in 1974 while we were still based in the police station, and Roger Goad, who was appointed early in 1975. Memories of our times together at Feltham flooded back; we even found ourselves playing the same jokes we'd pulled years ago, such as lightly filling in Roger's crossword puzzle when he wasn't looking.

The Bungalow made for a comfortable home: it had two large open-plan offices, a couple of largish workshops, a training area, restroom with television, showers, a duty officer's bunk, a communications and administration office, and a secure library. The library was stacked high with shelves and filing cabinets. Apart from housing the usual textbooks on explosives, munitions and IEDs, it was also a data centre because we were now part of the worldwide network of bomb information resources.

I was never sure who started the network but it certainly works well. Virtually every country now has its own Bomb Data Centre, interlinked by fax, telephone and computer to all the others around the world, which focuses principally on the IED: who is making it, where it is being used, how it is changing in design, construction and application. With only one or two exceptions, information is freely and readily shared (of the major Western countries only France is still reluctant to provide information about its bombs). International contact amongst explosives officers has also increased, to the extent that operators now ring each other within a short time of an unusual incident occurring on their territory.

This willingness to share vital information sometimes has its humorous side: when the Israelis heard of the IRA mortar attack on Downing Street the head of their Bomb Squad immediately rang me to see if it would help us to know the precautions they had worked out to thwart Scud attacks. Distorted news reports of the Downing Street incident had given the Israelis the impression that we'd encountered bombs the size of missiles rather than shells, hence the reference to Scuds. As a result of this conversation, IRA mortars became known as 'Spuds'.

Every day, by telephone, telex and international mail, we received news of incidents large and small, information about the few that made the headlines and the many that did not. Week by week, month by month, international co-operation slowly broadened and strengthened in the face of a threat which knew no borders.

Information exchange and compilation was an integral part of the day's routine. We had three shifts – one operating from 8 a.m.

to 4 p.m., another from 4 p.m. to 1 a.m., and the third from midnight to 8 a.m. (The one-hour extension of the middle shift and its overlap with the third shift was deliberate: experience showed that the IRA was very active between 10 p.m. and 1 a.m.) The shifts worked on a ten-day fortnight; we were fully operational for seven days (working at least fifty-six hours, Monday through Sunday), and then non-operational for three days of the following week. The four days off in the second week arose because explosives officers have to be on duty at weekends, do not have any prescribed meal breaks, and under civil service regulations are therefore entitled to time in lieu.

Non-operational days were not a time to put your feet up; Expos would be away from the Bungalow giving lectures to groups such as airport and Government department staff or out on visits to research establishments, forensic laboratories, or attending conferences. Paperwork could be inordinately time-consuming. As more and more countries came together in the exchange of bomb data, it was not unusual to receive eighty pages of information a day. You couldn't afford to miss it – who was to say that the next device you had to deal with would not be modelled on one previously encountered by another operator overseas?

As an Expo, you are required to fill in a report form in respect of every job, no matter how small. Normally, your report form is also the tasking form, a document intended to record the time of the incoming job, name of operator allocated, time of arrival at scene, nature of location, nature of incident, details of actual or suspected device. Only if a crime is suspected is a statement requested, and that may often be months later, or even years.

A copy of all tasking/report forms is left with our central office; the first thing every Expo does when arriving on duty is flick through those copies to see what has happened since he was last on duty. If anything of special note does occur, a further message is written on our wipe-off noticeboard, saying, for instance, 'All Expos to see message so-and-so.' If the content of this message is

unclassified, then it will be available at central office; if it is classi-
fied, it will be held within the secure library.

Having checked the messages, the Expo then checks his equipment. Range Rovers are shared between two Expos, one who is
operational and one who is not. On board the Range Rover is a
variety of equipment, some sophisticated, some fairly rudimentary,
particularly the hook and line – a long piece of light nylon rope
with various attachments. It can be used from a safe distance to
move a suspect bomb or things lying around it.

Also aboard the Range Rover is the disrupter; about 18 inches
long, it is a steel tube which fires a quantity of water by means of
an explosive cartridge. The velocity of the jet of water is so great
that when it hits a bomb it actually penetrates the interior and
disrupts the circuitry before the circuits can close. Disrupters are
used by EOD organizations throughout the world. They are
highly effective, but also lethal: the plastic plug which holds the
water in place will kill you if you are in the way and the recoil
kickback is about 40 yards. Expos will usually restrain it from
flying back that far by using a special stand or wedging it.

In addition there is a small explosives kit, a shotgun, and complete bomb suit. The suit is of limited value: its tremendous weight
makes walking difficult and, with bombs often tucked away in
awkward corners, its bulk inhibits effective operation. (A bomb suit
will only provide protection in certain kinds of incident anyway; if
you happen to be on top of more than a kilogram of high explosive
when it goes off, it will mean only that slightly bigger pieces of
your body will remain to be picked up.) For that reason, Expos
tend to wear flak jackets and bomb helmets; they may not afford
quite the protection of a full bomb suit but they are infinitely more
practical and provide good protection from fragments if a device
goes off while you are walking towards it.

Expos also wear fire-resistant clothing – because explosions are
invariably followed by a fire-ball – and boots. These would have
been useful some years earlier when, following an explosion at

Gieves & Hawkes in Savile Row, I went in to rescue an injured person, discovered it was a tailor's dummy, and then realized I was standing on a nail which had driven upwards through the sole of my heavy shoe, through my foot, and out through the leather upper.

Personal kit is down to each individual Expo: Stanley knife, screwdrivers, wire-cutters, even rose-pruners. The Expo also has his own small X-ray machine which now weighs less than 10 pounds. Used in conjunction with a Polaroid X-Ray plate, this enables an operator to see a positive image (as opposed to the hospital-style negative image) in less than thirty seconds. Finally there's the Wheelbarrow; though not carried on the Range Rover, it is available on demand.

Our new well-equipped premises with increased staffing was much needed: we were having to cover an area that extended from north of Oxford down to the south coast and the Isle of Wight, taking in the whole of Kent, Sussex, Essex and the rest of the Home Counties. The army was still tasked with handling CMD, and little if anything was happening outside the London metropolitan area, but there was nothing to suggest that terrorism wouldn't spread to the south-east.

Improvements in communications were well-nigh constant, and occasionally a boon to practical jokers. One night Ken Howorth and I were on the late-turn duty and the Hotline rang – the direct connection between the explosives officers and the Bomb Squad (now the Anti-Terrorist Branch of the Metropolitan Police). You could always tell which was the Hotline: it had a distinctive ring as well as a red flashing light on the top of the telephone. A call on the Hotline was always imperative; whatever you were doing at the time you had to get to that phone and answer as quickly as possible.

That night we were well prepared. I had my small portable tape unit with a standard recorded message:

'I'm sorry but there's no one here to take your call at the moment.

Please leave your message and we'll get back to you when we can. Please speak clearly and slowly after the tone.'

I picked up the Hotline and Ken held the recorder to the mouthpiece. He punched the start button and the message played. There was a brief silence and then we heard someone from the Bomb Squad: 'Christ Almighty! It's an Ansaphone. I've got a fucking Ansaphone. What the hell am I supposed to do *now*?'

Ken collapsed in hysterics. With some difficulty I told the Bomb Squad I was now answering for real. It took them a while to appreciate the joke.

In operational situations, too, humour frequently came into play – as in the case of Queen Victoria's statue, an impressive edifice sited directly outside Buckingham Palace. In response to a bomb warning, I found myself undertaking a nerve-wracking examination of the monument's hollow interior. It was dark, and uncomfortable, and so constricted that I had to remove my bomb helmet – at which point my unprotected skull came into sharp contact with a hidden inner protrusion.

I radioed through to my driver: 'Guess what: you're talking to the only living Englishman to have banged his head on Queen Victoria's clitoris.'

Back came the reply: 'Yes, well, I've got news for you: I'm looking at her face, and she most definitely is not amused.'

Unorthodox additions to standard-issue uniform were sometimes called for. On one occasion we took some lead plate which we'd been using to shield emissions from the X-ray unit and cut it up into small pieces. We then inserted a couple of them into the pockets of a protective tabard-style garment worn by one of our colleagues.

As the tabard was quite a weight to begin with, the lead ballast wasn't immediately noticeable. In fact, our 'victim' didn't even remark upon it – which encouraged the furtive addition of even more pieces of plate. Finally, the operator said: 'I must be growing old: every day this week my bomb jacket seems to have got heavier and heavier. It was so bad today I almost couldn't stand upright . . .'

The reconstitution of the old Feltham group had made life at the Bungalow even more pleasant and served as a release from the pressures of the hour; for Ken, Roger and me, wind-down time became almost a ritual. It wasn't something we could always manage because we weren't always on the same roster, but on those days when we came off duty together we'd sit in our office and open a bottle of Teacher's whisky and discuss everything from Roger's golf handicap to the state of the world. We would review the problems each of us had encountered during the day and the solutions we'd devised. Sometimes we would discuss the host of ideas put forward both by officials and the public.

In some ways the public showed more imagination. One suggestion in particular showed ambition as well as originality: a gentleman wrote to us suggesting that, as the government must still hold 'large stocks' of barrage balloons from the Second World War, we should use these to beat the bombers. Instead of risking life and limb every time we dealt with a suspect car, why not couple it up to two or three barrage balloons? If it did explode, it would already be high in the air and so only minimal damage would occur; if it didn't, we could all happily wait until the wind had blown it out over the Channel, where 'our gallant lads in the RAF could then shoot it down'.

I had great difficulty in composing a reply, not least because a vision kept dancing before my eyes of cars popping skywards like champagne corks above London. I explained that the capital's narrow streets made life awkward if you were trying to tie down barrage balloons: apart from anything else, the small army of technicians involved would also be at risk. There were other considerations, too: always assuming that the cars didn't smash into the nearest building on their way up, God alone knew what Air Traffic Control would say at Heathrow and Gatwick. As for the work of our gallant lads in the RAF, I had every faith in their expertise, but the consequences of failure would be horrendous: Anglo-French relations were unlikely to be improved if the French looked out of their windows one morning and saw their skies filled with IRA car bombs dangling from English barrage balloons. Still, as Roger pointed out, it might encourage them to start sharing their IED data with the rest of the world.

I thanked our correspondent for his idea. His good intentions had offered us the kind of moral support we valued.

Unlike in Northern Ireland, where all too often an ATO is reviled, intimidated and even attacked by the very people whose lives and property he is trying to save, in mainland Britain people are very appreciative of the Expo's role.

In the wake of one particularly horrifying incident in London, a group of old-age pensioners wrote to me as head of the Met's Explosives Office. These pensioners had decided that the price some of us were having to pay was too high: we had wives, families, small children. They, however, had had their lives.

Some of them, said the letter-writer, had a basic knowledge of explosives from their own days in the army. They would be more than delighted to undertake a crash course on bomb disposal. If they were killed, they would die knowing that they had already had the best years of their lives, and that in dying for their Queen and their country they were also saving the life of a younger man.

I have never read a more extraordinary letter than this. And I have rarely had such difficulty in composing a reply. Even now, it is difficult to put into words what I feel about the spirit of people such as this.

Unfortunately one occasionally has to deal with people who are less helpful. I was once called to Hammersmith Broadway; a suspect bomb was reported on platform four of the Underground Station. The station had been cleared, the staff and public kept outside, behind a cordon. In the empty foyer a Met police officer and a London Transport official briefed me and confirmed that no trains were running past that platform.

Above: Kensington Church Street, 29 August 1975, shortly after a bomb exploded and killed Roger Goad.

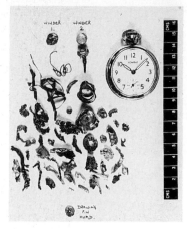

Right: Fragments of a Smith's Combat watch from the bomb. On the right is an undamaged watch for comparison purposes.

Above: Roger Goad's funeral,
5 September 1975. Peter is amongst
the mourners.

Below: A hoax bomb, used in an attempted bank raid.

Below: Peter and Ken Howorth, shortly before Ken was killed in 1981.

Above: The Wimpy
Bar, Oxford Street,
26 October 1981,
moments after the
bomb detonated.

Right: Harrods immediately after a car bomb exploded on 17 December 1983 killing five people.

Below: The remains of the Austin 1100 used in the attack.

Right: The Grand Hotel, Brighton, 12 October 1984.

Right: Nezar Hindawi's calculator bomb *before* being defuzed.

Below: The contents of Anne-Maria Murphy's bag spread out on a search table in Terminal 2, Heathrow, 17 April 1986.

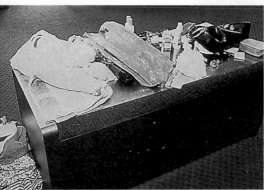

Below: Police comb the snow in St James's Park for mortar bomb fragments after the Downing Street attack, 7 February 1991.

Wearing my bomb helmet and flak jacket, and carrying my disrupter, portable X-ray and personal tool kit, I staggered across the foyer, looking less like a human being than a creature from a sci-fi film. At the ticket barrier I struggled to squeeze through. And then a voice said: 'Excuse me, sir. Can I see your ticket?'

I stared into the polite, impassive face of an elderly West Indian ticket collector. 'I haven't got a ticket.'

'Well, you can't come through without one.'

'But I'm here to defuze a bomb!'

'Oh no, sir. Not without a ticket.'

'Look,' I said. 'I am a bomb disposal officer. I have been summoned here because there's supposed to be a bomb on platform four. Now then; either you let me through or you can take my equipment down there yourself and *you* can defuze the thing.'

He considered this for a moment or two. Finally: 'All right, sir. You can go through ... just this once.'

During the IRA's letter-bomb campaign I again came across this kind of blinkered, unthinking officialdom. I was called to a house belonging to a public figure, a likely target for a letter bomb. I clambered out of the patrol car, walked up the steps and met a police sergeant who was guarding the front door. 'It's still in there,' he said. 'On a stand, in the hall.'

I thanked him and went in. I checked the hallway and glanced at the telephone directories and a postcard that had been left on the hallstand. There was no sign of any letter bomb. Someone must have taken the suspect mail away. I spun on my heel and wrenched open the front door. 'Sergeant, quick – is there another hall in this house?'

'No, sir ... ?' He stared blankly, bewildered by my question.

'There's no sign of a letter bomb in there.'

'There is, sir.' Bewilderment was replaced by certainty. 'It's on the hallstand.'

'Where?'

'On the top.'

'The only things on the hallstand are some phone books. Have you shoved the thing underneath them?'

'No. I didn't move it.' The stare had also gone now; he clearly thought I was blind or incompetent. 'It's on top of those telephone directories.'

I felt my pulse beginning to race. It had nothing to do with fear. 'The only thing on top of the directories is a postcard. A postcard.'

'Yes, sir. That's exactly it.'

'*What* is?'

'The postcard, sir.' He nodded. 'It's suspect.'

'The *postcard*?' I could hear my own disbelief echoing back to me. 'What the hell can be suspect about a *postcard*?'

'It was mailed in Dorking.'

The conversation came to an abrupt halt as I mentally replayed the reply. I took a deep breath. 'Sergeant, it is a postcard. A *postcard*. Never mind where it came from, never mind bloody Dorking, how can you get a bomb into a fucking *postcard*?'

The sergeant remained remarkably unfazed. 'It meets all the requirements, sir: it's unexpected, it has an oily stain on it, and it comes from someone unknown to the recipients. From Dorking, sir.'

I told him that (a) a letter bomb needs to be in a letter and (b) the letter needs to be at least one-eighth of an inch thick. He seemed unable to understand, although this may have been due to a certain lack of clarity on my part on account of the difficulty in speaking through gritted teeth.

Today the incident has a bizarre humour, but then it did not – we were working flat out to answer calls yet here I was diverted from my work by an utter buffoon. Even now, our conversation remains vivid; I have dealt with many stupid people in my time and many stupid situations but nothing has ever come close to the police sergeant and his damned postcard. It was for that reason that I broke my own cardinal rule: for the only time on any job I actually lost my temper.

Another instance of keenness defeating logic came when someone somewhere believed that a solution had been found to all our
problems: the Portable Concrete Garage.

In great secrecy, and at great expense, a trial was organized
by several Government departments to test the effectiveness of a
proposal that a six-inch-thick concrete box should be lowered on
to a suspect car to contain the effects of an explosion. Unfortunately, the organizers of the trial didn't bother to contact us. We'd
have told them that concrete garages are not particularly portable
and that in the middle of an IRA car bomb campaign the last thing
time or London's crowded streets allow is the slow passage of a
giant crane.

They headed for a quiet rural location, packed a car with 100
pounds of HE and manoeuvred a crane alongside to winch down
upon the car one extremely heavy and well-made concrete garage.
As soon as the garage covered the car they detonated the bomb.
The garage was completely destroyed, so much so that the roof
was never found. They had, in effect, created a giant hand-grenade.

We toasted the venture with happy irony in one of our wind-
down sessions, when the Teacher's came out and the glasses were
passed around. Sometimes our drivers joined us, sometimes we
had business to discuss. It was different from military life and yet
the old army camaraderie lived on, the sense of belonging to a
small and specialist group of people. We had learned our craft and
the army had served us well – in fact, Roger had so enjoyed it he'd
taken a Commission as a captain, which explained why, whenever
he made a particularly forceful remark during one of our off-duty
sessions, Ken would raise his arm in mock salute.

Those brief, infrequent evening sessions at the Bungalow were
only feasible when the pressure was off. When the quiet times
were over, the hours on the duty roster meant nothing: as long as
you had a job to complete, you stayed out on the street.

7

The IRA in London

=

On my first day at the Met I had sat wondering what kind of challenges the job would bring, anticipating that London would be quite different to Northern Ireland. Less than four weeks later I had to think again.

An Intelligence report arrived warning of a major car bomb attack or attacks by the IRA in London on 8 March. All five explosives officers were alerted for round-the-clock operation from 7 March. The metropolitan area was systematically scoured – hundreds of square miles of roads and streets and alleyways. The task was huge, the time short. To add to the problem there were strikes on British Rail and the London Underground. Never could industrial action have been so mistimed: at the very moment when we needed as few vehicles as possible in central London, parking restrictions had to be relaxed to cope with the massive influx of cars.

The Ford saloon was spotted by two alert officers from the Special Patrol Group. It was parked outside the Post Office in Broadway opposite New Scotland Yard. Unless you knew what to look for, nothing about the car suggested the nature of the threat. But it was mistagged: the number plates did not tie in with the model year. The SPG officers carefully examined the plates and saw evidence of tampering: screwdriver scratches, slight mispositioning, some slackness. They also saw an air freshener.

Geoffrey and I arrived in an area police car. He had been up all night whereas my day was only just beginning. We examined the Ford and looked particularly at the boot.

'What d'you think?' Geoffrey said. 'There's something wrong with the lock.' He pointed to the dented key-slot.

I didn't like the look of it either: it could be accidental damage or it could be evidence of some kind of booby-trap. We backed off. The luggage compartment would have to be checked but lifting the boot-lid was out of the question; we'd need to get access via the Ford's interior.

I jiggled the lock on the nearside rear door, released the catch and eased the door open. The smell of nitrobenzene was overpowering: you'd have needed a dozen air fresheners to defeat it; the Ford had only one. Either it had been in the vehicle when it was acquired by the bombers or they'd been too mean and too stupid to realize that nitrobenzene isn't masked by a single whiff of Forest Glade or Alpine Mountain.

With each moment that passed, the time was drawing nearer to detonation. It could be in a minute or it could be an hour – only the bombers knew.

In the days before cars had fireproof internal rear bulkheads, the easiest way to get into a locked boot was by lifting out the rear seat squab and clambering in. Today it isn't possible; in 1973, it was. I made to lift up the squab and almost sustained a hernia: it was so heavy I wondered if it was somehow bolted into place. It didn't make sense for a section of seating to be as immovable as this. Carefully, cautiously, I lifted it up, looked underneath, and saw a gleaming mass of polythene bags packed with explosive. Not only that, they'd removed the springs from the squab and packed its interior with explosive as well.

One pound of high explosive is sufficient to blow a car to

pieces; the dozens of bags crammed into the back of this vehicle looked as though they weighed 5 pounds each. If this thing blew it would make Broadway look like a battle zone.

We decided to shift some of the bags. If the bomb went off while we were standing next to it, one bag or one hundred wouldn't make much difference to us: we'd both be dead. But less explosive meant less likelihood of death or injury to the people still being evacuated from nearby buildings. It would also give Geoffrey and me a chance to find the bomb's initiating system.

I glanced around the incident scene; there seemed to be a lot of people near by. Familiarity would soon bring a greater understanding of danger, but London had had little experience of car bombs before 1973; the police at the scene had no idea of what happens when a vehicle containing over 180 pounds of HE blows up.

Geoffrey and I began removing the bags one by one. I tested their weight; each was around 5 pounds and each contained Co-op. The mixture had not been used in London before but I'd seen enough of it in Northern Ireland to know that this home-made concoction was as powerful as it was sensitive – shock and friction could set this stuff off. We ran with them and set them down on the other side of the road, far enough away not to be set off by the detonation of the main charge.

I wasn't sure if Geoffrey was fully cognizant of the properties of Co-op. I'd once taken a sample of the stuff to a Home Office laboratory specializing in explosives analysis and been met by a very superior scientist. Oh no, said the scientist, there must be some mistake. A mixture of nitrobenzene and sodium chlorate would be far too sensitive to handle. The very idea was unworkable. I felt like asking him to put it in a memo to the IRA. They'd blown up half of Belfast with Co-op mix but perhaps if the Home Office told them it was too dangerous to use they'd pack it in.

The Ford's cargo was gradually diminishing: twelve bags ... fifteen ... twenty. I suddenly looked up at the façade of New Scotland Yard, the headquarters of the Metropolitan Police itself, and saw that all the windows were filled with faces looking down at us.

A figure was moving about behind one of the pillars near the main entrance. 'You!' I shouted. 'That man lurking behind the pillar!' Twenty-three years of army life endowed it with all the force of a barrack-square command. 'You get inside and get those stupid bastards away from the windows! If this thing goes off they'll be wearing glass for the rest of their lives.'

The figure hesitated briefly, then vanished inside. He turned out to be a very senior officer indeed, which probably explained why the faces at the window disappeared so rapidly.

With half the bags removed we at last found the core of the car bomb: 40 pounds of commercial explosive – Gelamex or Frangex. The bombers had obviously intended for this to go off first: though not strictly necessary, it would provide so powerful an explosive boost that the home-made stuff – which might otherwise perform erratically – would all go up in one enormous bang.

The commercial charge was laced with Cordtex detonating cord; it ran down and underneath the rear carpet to the well beneath the front passenger seat. Geoffrey slowly eased out a box that had been hidden there, its external detonators connected up to the Cordtex. The box contained a modified alarm clock, terminal and battery. The bomb had been designed to explode between two and three o'clock that afternoon; though we hadn't known it when we'd started our work, we'd had a minimum of four hours in hand.

It would have been comforting to be more exact, but that wasn't possible because of the modification to the clock: if the hour hand alone is used, a bomber can have almost twelve hours' grace; with only the minute hand, about sixty minutes. As I knew from experience, there were even clocks which had both hands removed, evidence of what came to be known amongst bomb men as 'the Paddy Factor'; a clock with no hands is about as much use as a bomb with no explosive. In this instance the bombers had removed the minute hand and worked with the hour hand alone.

Geoffrey neutralized the timer and removed the detonators from the box; I removed the Cordtex from the charge. We stepped back and contemplated our handiwork. But even as we gathered our things together, all hell was breaking loose around London: more suspect car sightings, more alerts, more urgent messages over the communications net. I suspected that someone somewhere in authority knew how many bombs there were but had decided not to tell us. Not that it mattered; throughout that morning we were perpetually on the move. Geoffrey went home after a very long night and an exhausting morning; I continued with Andy Clarke.

At this time explosives officers always worked in pairs. It was – and still is – army practice but in civil operations had ceased to make much sense. The army's theory was that two heads are better than one. But in the army only one man went forward to deal with the bomb; in the Met, both men dealt with it. It seemed a particularly stupid way of doing things; if anything went wrong with an army operation, only one man might be killed; with a Met operation, both explosives officers would die.

Early that afternoon we were tasked to a car in Dean Stanley Street outside the headquarters of the British Forces' Broadcasting Service. By now the day had become a kind of blur. Like us, Don Henderson and Ronnie Wilson and an army team from Hounslow were criss-crossing central London. Many of the jobs were never logged because there simply wasn't time: you reached a car, popped the window, searched it, and raced off to the next job. London had never seen urban terrorism on this scale before.

The car was a Vauxhall Viva. We looked through the window, saw an Irish 2p piece on one of the seats and an air freshener. I checked my watch; this vehicle bore all the hallmarks of the New Scotland Yard car bomb – which meant that its timer could be running to an identical schedule. It was now 2.35 p.m. Whether we lived or died would depend on the accuracy with which the clock had been set and the speed with which we could deal with the device.

I broke the Vauxhall's rear offside window, reached in, killed the interior light and unlocked the door. As before, the smell of nitrobenzene almost swamped me. I unlocked the other door for Andy and then carefully lifted up the rear carpet. Twin leads of detonating cord bound together with adhesive tape ran from the rear to a small box in the recess under the front seat: so far same design, same bomb and, very likely, the same timetable.

Ideally, I wanted to disconnect the detonator, but it was under the front seat and couldn't be reached without moving the clock box. To touch a timer mechanism which is close to running out is to invite disaster: the slightest movement can cause the contacts to close, which would complete the bomber's work for him.

The only option we were left with was to cut the detonating cords. This would have to be done with exceptional care, but if I pressed down on the leads to keep them steady while Andy did the cutting, we should be OK.

'We'll have to cut,' I told him. I manoeuvred awkwardly, half-in and half-out of the car; I wished Vauxhall hadn't made the thing so small. 'I'll hold the leads firm, you cut.'

Andy hesitated and patted his pockets. 'I haven't a knife.'

'Doesn't matter. Use a pair of wire-cutters.'

More futile checking of pockets. 'I haven't any tools with me.'

Marvellous. I had my tools in my pockets but couldn't reach them because of the way I was positioned; having already pressed down on the detonating cords it would be unwise to disturb them again.

Andy disappeared to fetch a cutting tool. I remained stuck in a car holding the detonating leads of a bomb with a very short fuze indeed. I waited, and waited. The seconds seemed like hours. Finally I let go of the cords.

Getting out of the car was as slow-motion as everything else: my body weight had exerted pressure on the Vauxhall's suspension; removing that weight meant an easing of the pressure and this could cause the car to rock – highly undesirable in these circumstances.

I stood upright and breathed slowly, steadily. I reached in my pockets for my own cutting tools, bent down again, held the leads – hoping to God that the steadying effect of just one hand would be sufficient to prevent any vibration from travelling to the detonating mechanism – and then severed them.

The Vauxhall was packed with about 120 pounds of high explosive. I removed the rear seat complete with its explosive, went back in and dealt with the clock box and the electric detonator. I checked the clock; once again the bomber had used the hour hand alone to set the time. It was now almost 2.40 p.m.; although pinpoint accuracy is never possible with a one-hand clock, it seemed likely I'd completed the job with less than ten minutes to spare.

Andy returned. I told him what I'd done and left him to get on with the job of unpacking the main charge from within the rear seat. I was concerned about the timing on other car bombs. I ran into the British Forces' Broadcasting building, grabbed a telephone and rang our Control Office. 'If there are any more bombs, my advice is that the team should stay laid back. We're running out of time.'

As I cradled the telephone, a distinctive rumbling noise reached my ears: a car bomb in Great Scotland Yard, only a short distance from Whitehall and the Ministry of Defence, had just gone off. A few moments later, although I didn't hear it because of the traffic noise and the Belfast-style overlay of sirens and alarms, another car bomb exploded outside the Old Bailey.

Both bombs were similar to those at Broadway and Dean Stanley Street. Both went off with enormous force and caused enormous damage. Thankfully, the Great Scotland Yard explosion neither killed nor injured anyone; the army team which had been dealing with it were well away from the vehicle at the time of detonation, in the process of removing the detonating cords with a very long hook and line arrangement.

Though the Old Bailey car had been spotted, the area was still in the process of being cleared and the other Met team was still en route to the scene. The explosion injured over a hundred people

The next day Andy and I were again teamed together and tasked
to another suspect car. The experience proved one too many: being
ex-Northern Ireland, I never opened a car door without making
certain checks beforehand. In any event I always pulled out the
interior light after popping one of the windows. Bombers had been
known to link their devices to a car's interior light circuit.

Andy was alongside as I popped one of the windows. 'Peter,'
he said, 'there's no need to do that. The car's not locked.' And with
that he opened the door.

When we'd finished the job I went back to Cannon Row and
sought out the Chief Superintendent. From now on, I said, I would
only work on my own. I did not wish to work with anyone else.
He didn't argue.

After the car bombs came the incendiaries – dozens of them.
They were as simple as they were effective: a cigarette packet
containing a small quantity of incendiary material, a battery and a
modified wristwatch. The igniter was based on the kind of hot-wire
device used to light domestic gas stoves.

The IRA targeted London's major department stores: Harrods,
Austin Reed, Liberty, Swan & Edgar, and Harvey Nichols. The
damage was caused not so much by the fires as by the in-store
sprinkler systems. The campaign reached its peak in the summer
of '73 when I found myself in more department stores in a week
than the average shopper might visit in a year.

The disruptive effects of the incendiary were monitored by the
IRA and the lessons well learned; two decades later, in 1991 and
1992, incendiaries were again used for a major campaign. The
intervening years brought some modifications: cassette tape carriers containing timer chips rather than wristwatch parts were used.

Overreaction by the relevant authorities to the latest threat of
the incendiary was doubtless expected by the IRA and certainly
exploited to the full: it took only a very small device left in a
railway carriage or a London Underground train to ensure
maximum publicity, the dislocation of public services, and the dis-

ruption of the economic life of the capital. Endangering life o
property was not the prime motive.

The closing down of complete sections of a city's thoroughfare
or its transport systems merely because a small fire might puff int
life is unjustified – not least because it is precisely what the terror
ists have intended. The chances of encountering an incendiary o
the London Underground are infinitely less than having one'
fingers caught between the sliding doors. The prospect of injury i
even more remote: if an incendiary went off under the cushion o
which you were sitting you'd have to be extremely slow to suffe
more than a warm posterior. Unless you're holding an incendiar
in your hand with your face pressed close to it, serious injury i
well-nigh impossible. The explosive content is not much more tha
that of an ordinary box of household matches.

Unfortunately there was soon a deliberate policy shift by th
IRA which meant that innocent people became a direct target.

It was Thursday, 23 August 1973. I'd been tasked to the radi
mast at Crystal Palace, where some sort of package had bee
spotted. En route, though, I was diverted to Baker Street Unde
ground Station: someone had found a bag which they thoug
contained a bomb – they'd opened it up and seen what appeare
to be an alarm clock with wires attached.

I didn't discount it but was highly sceptical: no matter ho
well-intentioned, the finder very probably had an overacti
imagination; there was no history of the IRA leaving packa
bombs in London's public places.

My driver switched on the police car's headlights and bl
beacons and used the two-tone horn to carve a way through t
5 p.m. rush-hour traffic. They'd closed the Underground Statio
People were milling around outside, waiting for the place
reopen. A police officer led me across the station foyer and tick
concourse and pointed to the bag, one of those Swinging Lond
affairs with a huge Union Jack on either side. It was leaning agair
the window of a chemist's shop.

The shop had a dual-aspect frontage: one set of windows looked out on to the concourse, the other set on to Baker Street. I moved in closer, thinking about the positioning: unlikely though it still seemed, if this was a bomb it was certainly in an ideal position. An explosion at this time would send glass scything through the crowds of home-going commuters.

I looked up from the bag to find myself staring into hundreds of faces pressing up against the windows on the Baker Street side. Clearly, we still had a lot to learn about crowd control and safety zones. I told the police to get everyone as far back as possible immediately and then examined the bag.

The man who'd reported it had been correct. This was no wild flight of imagination but a modified alarm clock with wires connected to an Ever Ready PP9 battery, a detonator and about 3 pounds of plaster gelatine (a very powerful high explosive based on nitroglycerine). The clock was set to fire the bomb at 5.37 p.m., the peak of the rush hour when the death and injury toll would have been at its highest. I did a rapid evaluation of the circuitry, worked out what I thought was its probable path, cut the detonator wires and then cautiously and carefully unpacked the rest of the bag.

I was in the middle of doing so when what had been a completely deserted concourse suddenly filled with people: a train had come in and disgorged its passengers. Horrified, I watched as more and more people stepped off the escalator and surged towards me. Utter chaos ensued; quite how London Transport could close off one of its stations yet still have a train-load of passengers coming in was beyond my comprehension. London indeed had a lot to learn.

Eventually the concourse was cleared again. I finished unpacking the explosive and the IRA phoned in a bomb warning. Had it not been for a passerby sensing something suspicious about the bag, we would only have had this warning to go on. At the height of London's rush hour the amount of time allowed by that warning was unlikely to have been enough.

The Baker Street attack was the first example in the current IRA campaign of indiscriminate bombing of the mainland civilian population. Its conception marked a change in policy and its outcome a change of tactics: after Baker Street the IRA took care to hide its bombs from plain sight. In Belfast the population had been taught by long experience never to go anywhere near a suspect package; in London, in 1973, members of the public were less circumspect in their approach.

The Baker Street attack also ushered in a policy of bomb warnings which neither public nor media have as yet fully comprehended: the system of 'coded calls'. Even today the public think that if the IRA telephone a warning and accompany it with a code word, then the authorities should immediately jump to it in the certain knowledge that the message is not a hoax. This is not so. IRA killers do not have some sort of code book with a list of authorized and non-authorized words, and nor do the people they choose to call. Which means the only time you can be sure you have received an authentic warning is *after* you've found an authentic bomb or *after* it has gone off.

From 1973 onwards it was not unusual for the Metropolitan Police to receive up to 200 hoax calls a *day*, at least fifty of them with alleged code words. The hoaxers read that this was IRA practice and so invented their own; we had no way of finding out what was real and what was not.

Even the authentic warnings were not what they seemed: many incorporated a code word which had been heard before but omitted to give a precise location and/or time; others would use a nonsense word but be slightly more specific about location and timing. While it is in the IRA bombers' interest to pretend to the public that they always warn of a bomb, it is not in their interest to provide full and accurate details. The warning system is an integral part of the terrorism campaign and warnings are worded in such a way that vital information is withheld in order to confuse the authorities and divert blame away from the bombers.

Unfortunately there are people in the UK, Europe, Australia and the USA who actually believe the propaganda of terrorism, who are conned by the heroic myth of the IRA. Even the media still inadvertently contribute to the myth of the bombers' invincibility. For instance Semtex, a commercial explosive, is said by many a newspaper which should know better to be five, ten, fifteen, even twenty times more powerful than TNT. The truth is, Semtex is 1.3 times more powerful: 10 ounces of the stuff equals 13 ounces of TNT.

An ordinary plastic explosive, Semtex is made in Czechoslovakia and comprises the manufacturer's own RDX (cyclo-trimethylene-trinitramine), PETN (pentaerythritol tetranitrate) and plasticizer. It was first assembled in the 1960s when the manufacturer was supplying PETN and RDX for the filling of military shells. At the end of the production run they wondered what to do with the surplus. Thus Semtex became the Woodbine of all explosives (English Woodbine cigarettes were popularly believed to be filled with the sweepings from the cigarette-factory floor).

A pound of RDX or a pound of PETN has virtually the same explosive power as a pound of Semtex. The fact that the IRA got their hands on it never endowed the terrorists with some 'super-powerful' weapon; they used it not because they were clever but because Libya's Colonel Gaddafi gave it to them by the ship-load in full knowledge of its intended use.

In the wake of the Lockerbie bombing, representatives of the manufacturers of Semtex came to Britain and offered to incorporate within the explosive an element which would give off a distinctive smell – providing that the British-manufactured PE4 (Plastic Explosive 4) was likewise modified. In making the offer, the Semtex people were aware of the fact that, like the British PE4, the American C4 and the French Plastique, Semtex is capable of both civil and military application; the addition of a tracer element would seriously inhibit any wartime use because sabotage and demolition charges could be detected.

The Semtex representatives could not have been more open, more honest, or more helpful. But though Britain was delighted with the initiative, it refused to make the very modifications that it wished others to undertake. The offer was rejected. Czechoslovakian Semtex, like British PE4, is still extremely difficult to detect.

Yet another phase of 1973's undeclared war on London by the IRA was heralded by the letter bomb: between 21 and 25 August eleven were sent through the post. Only two of them detonated and these, thankfully, were only partial detonations; we caught up with all the others before they could do any harm.

The bombs had various classic hallmarks: oily stains on the front, similar handwriting of the names and addresses. Unfortunately once again we found ourselves having to deal with hoaxes – which dramatically increased after television showed what a letter bomb actually looked like. Though this kind of publicity was bound to encourage the idiot hoaxers, I approved of the TV coverage because knowledge is armour.

In February 1974 Reginald Maudling, a former Cabinet Minister, unwittingly opened a letter bomb at his country home. Fortunately only the detonator went off, injuring his thumb while ripping out the envelope and scattering small pieces of the unexploded charge across his carpet.

Mr Maudling was unable to tell me anything significant, which wasn't surprising; what was curious, though, was the state of the room.

The Explosives Office had by now handled dozens of letter-bomb incidents and where only the detonator had gone off there was always plenty of explosive material to collect for forensic examination. Here there was very little: a few crumbs inside the envelope, a few crumbs on the floor. A letter bomb usually contained around 3 ounces of nitroglycerine-based explosive; where was the rest of the charge?

And then Mr Maudling's little white dog came into the room. By its movements I knew immediately what was wrong: it was suffering from an extreme case of NG head, obviously the result of having eaten the scattered explosive when no one was looking. The dog died a day or so later; the Irish Republican Army had won yet another glorious victory.

10 p.m., Friday 29 August 1975: my driver had picked me up from home to take me to the Bungalow. Almost immediately the call had come through: suspect bomb, Kensington Church Street. I went on the air and said I'd take it; I'd be there in less than fifteen minutes.

I had no sooner settled deeper into the seat of the Range Rover, ready for a high-speed dash through the streets of the city, when Roger Goad came on. He had been doing a job in Slough and was now heading back into London. He was within three or four minutes of Kensington. I advised Base Control that Roger was taking the job and that I would go on to Cannon Row.

10.10 p.m.: the third message of the evening came through. It was Roger's driver, Peter Clary. There'd been an explosion. Roger was dead.

The Range Rover swerved through the mesh of side streets, the lights on, beacons flashing, horn blaring.

We stopped near the top of Kensington Church Street, unable to make any further headway because of the crowds and the cars and the cordons.

A lone police constable was almost lost in the chaos. He was young and he was doing his best but communications were a shambles: he had no way of making contact with Incident Control. I tried getting through from the Range Rover but it was no good – the radios were jammed with calls.

I shouldered my way past the crowd and was motioned through by the PC. I walked into the open space and the silence beyond the cordon. Roger was still lying there, out on the street.

I knelt down beside him, unaware of the fragments of glass that dug into my knees. Black shadow pooled between the orange street lamps. The nearby shop windows were dark. Roger would have died instantaneously. He hadn't been wearing any protective gear but it wouldn't have made the slightest difference: the injuries were massive. I examined his body, not thinking of Roger as he used to be, as the friend I had last spoken to only fifteen minutes earlier. Roger was gone. The injuries would help to explain why.

Eventually I straightened up. I had assessed which parts of the body had sustained the greatest damage and thus the greatest impact. I could now visualize Roger at the moment when the explosion occurred: he must have been hunched down when either the timer ran out or something which he was touching initiated detonation.

I moved away from the body and stepped over the K Shoes sign. The bomb had been in the shoe-shop doorway; its force had reduced the façade and interior to matchwood. Ladies' and gents' shoes lay negligently on the pavement and the road.

The night fled by. Even if I'd had any inclination to brood over Roger's death, time was against it. There were unsubstantiated rumours of a second device, and everyone in the area had started seeing bombs everywhere. I found myself rushing to and fro between the main incident scene and the nearby streets. By night's end I'd dealt with three jobs within the cordons and eight beyond. Seven of these proved routine; the eighth was only a very small box. It sat in the shadowed doorway of a shop in Notting Hill Gate, just outside the cordoned area. It was like the sort of box you would carry a cake in.

I moved in close. I wanted to get a detailed X-ray of the lower interior of the box. If some mechanism or configuration of circuitry and switches had been responsible for detonating the bomb that killed Roger (rather than the timer running out), it must have been deep down, hidden from plain sight – and not easily captured on X-ray by the portable scanner.

I tried to get the X-ray into exact alignment, but there was very little space within the narrow doorway. In the end I finished up with my head almost touching the floor, my face a few centimetres from the box. The box moved.

There was only a second or so in which to register it: the rustling sound, the sudden movement, the cold black terror that bit with heart-stopping suddenness. Only a second or so, and then I was staring at – a mouse.

One of us had to be more terrified of the other, but you couldn't have said which. The mouse didn't so much turn and run as vanish. I was left taking deep measured breaths, my face still almost touching the box.

It didn't take long to finish the X-raying and prove that the cake box was empty except for a few crumbs. I didn't feel self-conscious about completing the work; better to proceed as planned than wind up under a headstone reading Here Lies Peter Gurney, Frightened By A Mouse Then Killed By A Bomb.

I packed my things together, headed back to Kensington Church Street and supervised the evidence search (the systematic sweeping up and collecting of all materials from the outermost periphery of the blast to the seat of the explosion). Daybreak came at 5.30 a.m.

The day that followed felt heavy and muted. An increasingly weary disbelief filled the Bungalow. We waited for the forensic report to come through, for the explanation of why Roger died.

Several explosives officers flatly refused to believe it could have been anything other than the timer running out, that bad luck rather than misjudgement had caused Roger's death. I could understand the general feeling: if you convinced yourself that the timer was responsible, you could take comfort from the fact that the chances of being caught in a similar situation were very small. But if you admitted that Roger had been killed by an anti-handling device, you were acknowledging your own vulnerability: if someone as professional and as experienced as Roger could be killed by an IED then so, too, could you.

You had to believe in your own skill. Self-doubt was dangerous. You would die if your luck ran out but you would not die because a bomb had outwitted you. Yes, every device had the potential to kill you, but you knew that and legislated for it just as you contended with your own nature, your own fallibilities.

So we waited for the forensic report, and got on with the duties of the day. There was no weeping for Roger because explosives officers rarely if ever show emotion; it's in the nature of the job that you are ruled by your brain rather than your heart. There was sadness for Roger's wife, Maureen, and his two young daughters, a kind of shared awareness of their pain and loss. There were moments when I would glance up, suddenly conscious of the fact that I'd been about to say something that related to Roger as if he were still with us. But those moments were rare, and rapidly passed.

The forensic scientists concluded that the timer had closed and initiated detonation of the bomb. The report didn't alter the sadness of Roger's loss, but it did make a difference to those who lived on: at the Bungalow, the deep and unspoken anxiety felt by several officers was replaced by an equally deep and unspoken sense of relief. Roger died because his luck ran out. Ironically, as an explanation for a death, it was the only explanation that could be lived with.

8

Return to Sender

An explosives officer doesn't normally keep track of the progress of a criminal investigation. Incidents come and go, some of them hoaxes, some false alarms, and some of them the real thing. You deal with the situation, make your report, and log it for use in the event of a future prosecution. Many of the jobs to which you've been tasked tend to slip from memory as the years go by; some do not.

On 14 December 1977 a suspect parcel was delivered to the Croydon home of a local councillor renowned for some fairly controversial views. The police were called in and what followed became one of the most intriguing criminal cases I have ever encountered.

The parcel was waiting for me in the Charge Room when I arrived at New Addington Police Station. It was unusual to be dealing with a suspect device inside a police station, but the officers who had brought it in had assumed – dangerously so, in my view – that the thing would only go off when it was opened.

I started X-raying the parcel. It was a bomb all right, but the X-ray image showed what appeared to be an initiatory system based on a photo-electric cell. The container was covered in smooth wrapping paper; the cell seemed to be just inside the container.

Obviously, the instant you removed the wrapping paper and opened the box, light would flood in and be detected by the cell.

I studied the X-ray of the wiring circuit and identified what I thought was the final arming connection. Slowly and carefully I made a cut in the wrapping paper just above that connection. Only then did I see the second layer of wrapping paper. It was black.

It didn't make sense: why would anyone want to wrap up a parcel bomb in two layers of paper? And why black paper? Black wrapping was found on photographic paper, on materials which had to be shielded from the light . . . Realization suddenly dawned.

Instead of assuming how the bomb would function, I should have taken another X-ray at right angles to the first. This would have shown that the photo-electric cell was actually in a cleverly fashioned recess on top of the container, positioned in such a way that the action of *tearing off the paper* would initiate detonation. The paper was black to prevent light getting in, and I'd just cut through it.

All these thoughts flashed quickly through my head. Within split-seconds of cutting the black paper I had understood its significance, visualized how the bomb would function, and realized the scale of my error. I had pressed my hand down on to the cut and, as both the parcel and I were still intact, everything seemed OK.

But now what? I was standing in New Addington Police Station with a parcel bomb which would very likely explode if I took my hand off it. If I didn't take my hand off I wouldn't be able to deal with it. The bomb and I had just become inseparable.

I used my free hand to fumble for my radio and called my driver. I asked him to get hold of the station duty officer; I needed a totally blacked-out police cell.

The cell led directly off the Charge Room so I was able to watch my driver and a young police constable as they used heavy fabric and adhesive tape to shut out all the available light. The cell window required special care; the young policeman smiled apologetically at me. 'Excuse me, sir,' he said, 'but I wondered . . . Could you give us a hand to cover this thing up?'

I smiled back and told him I thought that might be a little inadvisable. 'This thing I'm holding. If I remove my hand, the light could set it off.' He stared at the way my hand was clamped over the package and swallowed hard.

Finally the cell was ready and I went into pitch blackness. There was no way of telling if this was overkill or not because the performance of a photo-electric cell is variable and adjustable: it may take only a glimmer of light to set it off or it may need a flashbulb. I didn't know how the bomber had adjusted the thing and I certainly didn't intend to make any more assumptions.

I set the package down on what felt like the cell bed. I had already taken care to memorize the X-ray image so now it was merely a case of locating the photo-electric cell and cutting the correct leg wire.

So much for the theory. The practice proved a little different: I was wearing surgeon's gloves, working in total darkness, and using a roll of Sellotape for insulation purposes. The bomb was on a bed still covered by a woolly blanket. The Sellotape finished up stuck to the blanket, to me, to my wire-cutters and to the bomb. Moreover, if I allowed these problems to interfere with my mental image of the X-ray then I'd lose complete track of the bomb's circuitry. I seemed to be in the darkness of the New Addington Police Station cell for a very long time.

Eventually the job was done: I cut the correct wire, insulated its ends, and disentangled myself from what had seemed to be the world's woolliest blanket.

Subsequent analysis of the device showed that it contained around 1¼ pounds of gunpowder with an initiatory system based on a photo-electric cell, thyristor, and four modified torch bulbs acting as hot-wire igniters. The circuit, which lacked any kind of safety mechanism, was capable of functioning on exposure to light.

For me, this was the end of the story. Detective Inspector

Stephenson and Detective Constable Reilly from the Met's Anti-Terrorist Branch were now drafted in. The latter was a local man with extensive local knowledge, a factor which was to be of crucial significance to the outcome of the case.

On 2 January 1978 an explosive device was discovered at the offices of a charitable organization in Horsham, Surrey, and rendered safe by a colleague of mine from the Explosives Office. The device bore a strong resemblance to the one I had so recently dealt with: it contained a similar photo-electric cell and thyristor initiatory system as well as a four-torch-bulb hot-wire igniter arrangement. The charge was bigger, though – almost 3 pounds of home-made explosive in a 1-litre solvent tin. Analysis also showed something else: mixed in with the explosive were fragments of glass from a 4-ounce Nescafé coffee jar. Marks had been made on the glass with a black felt-tip pen.

It seemed that both devices had been designed by the same bomb-maker. His intended victims had had lucky escapes so far. The investigation was stepped up and the police learned that the photo-electric cells had come from a batch of 115,000 and the thyristors from a batch of 20,000. Both the cells and the thyristors had been sold by a shop in London's Edgware Road. As for the torch bulbs, they were traced to Boots in Croydon.

While the laborious procedure of interviewing and statement-taking continued, Detective Constable Reilly happened to spend some off-duty time on a shopping trip to Croydon. When he saw some graffiti on the wall of a town-centre multi-storey car park, he remembered that there had previously been a complaint to the police about the vandalism; he went to check it for any clues. The graffiti was vehemently anti-abortionist, and Reilly remembered that this same wall had earlier been covered with graffiti denouncing the fluoridation of the local water supplies – graffiti in similar handwriting. As he looked at the way the individual letters were formed, Reilly realized that the last time he had seen handwriting like this was on the parcel bombs – bombs aimed at people who had, at one time or another, advocated more easily obtainable abortions.

It was not, thought Reilly, a coincidence, but it did not provide any clue to the writer's identity. This was sought by the police in the readers' letters pages of the local paper, which had, over a period of time, printed a variety of letters from a variety of readers on fluoridation and abortion. Only one correspondent, however, had written to express opposition on both topics. The letters were signed T. D. Lascelles.

On 10 January 1978 two detectives called at a house only a mile or so from New Addington Police Station. They were shown into Thomas David Lascelles's workroom. It was clean and tidy and contained a number of coffee jars with black felt-tip pen marks. In a box of rubbish the detectives found pieces of broken glass. Eventually something else was discovered: a 300-page diary detailing the author's activities during the previous year. Elegantly written in the style of Samuel Pepys, the diary documented the eloquent concern which became a deadly obsession, and the chilling and sad disintegration of a brilliant mind – the mind of a seventeen-year-old schoolboy.

Thomas David Lascelles admitted responsibility for the two bombs as well as a number of other attempted incendiary incidents in and around Croydon. He spoke calmly and clearly and even congratulated the arresting officers on the efficiency of their investigation.

I saw Lascelles from across a hushed Old Bailey Courtroom in July 1978. He sat quietly, impassively, a well-groomed and soberly dressed young man from a loving home. It was not difficult to believe that he had demonstrated an IQ of 160 at eight years old. Legal argument centred not so much on whether Lascelles was responsible for his actions as whether his psychopathic condition was treatable within the meaning of the Mental Health Act. Ultimately, he was saved from detention in a mental institution for an indefinite period of time but given six life sentences, one for each of the crimes as charged, in order to keep him away from the public.

In December 1988, eleven years after I grappled with his bomb in the cell at New Addington Police Station, Lascelles was found hanged in his cell at Kingston Prison, Portsmouth.

Today bombings account for over fifty per cent of all terrorist incidents worldwide; kidnapping and hostage-taking account for only around fifteen per cent. The Cold War is over, and preoccupations with 'the Bomb' have diminished, yet the threat of death and destruction from devices of infinitely less explosive power has, paradoxically, never been higher.

At an international conference hosted by the FBI and attended by EOD professionals from throughout the world, the keynote address (given by a member of the Office of the Ambassador at Large for Counter-Terrorism, US Department of State) opened thus:

> There are memorial plaques in the State Department lobby listing the names of American diplomats who died in the line of duty since 1776.
>
> When I joined the Foreign Service, twenty years ago, there were eighty-one names on those plaques. All but seven died from earthquakes, plagues and other non-purposeful causes.
>
> But during the last twenty years, seventy-three additional names have been added to those plaques. In other words, for the first 190 years of our nation's existence, we lost embassy personnel to violent death about once every twenty-seven years. Since I joined the Foreign Service, we have averaged one such loss every ninety days.

Terrorism is encountered everywhere, as I discovered for myself far from the Met's usual beat.

The story began in Malatya, a city in eastern Turkey, in 1978, when a parcel bomb killed the Mayor and his daughter. A description of the parcel was issued over Turkish radio and, by chance, was heard by the recipient of a second parcel bomb: the Chief of Police of a community not far from Malatya. What happened then was bizarre to say the least: as the parcel actually featured the sender's address, the Police Chief marked it IADE (acronym for the Turkish version of 'Return To Sender') and promptly put it back in the post, knowing what it contained. Efforts to deliver it failed because the address in Ankara was fictitious. Stuck with a parcel they couldn't deliver, the postal authorities decided to contact the addressee to see if he could help them. They rang the Police Chief. He told them it was a bomb. The parcel was hastily transported to Ankara's main police station, where no one seemed to know what to do with it; though their EOD operators examined it, they felt they were not capable of dealing with such a device.

By coincidence, Sir Lawrence Byford, an inspector of constabulary and a former chief constable of Lincolnshire, happened to be carrying out a police inspection that day in Ankara at the request of the Turkish government. During a tour of the main police station, he was advised not to go into one particular cell. As there seemed no good reason not to, and as he was, after all, acting at the request of the Government, he pushed open the door and went in to discover three parcels lying on the floor.

'What are these parcels doing here?' he asked.

'We think they're bombs.'

'Bombs? What are you doing with bombs in a police station? How are you going to deal with them?'

'We don't know.'

Byford rushed to the telephone and, as a result, I found myself boarding an aircraft to Turkey less than twenty-four hours later with instructions to defuze the devices.

As it turned out, two of the parcels were innocuous; the third contained the peripatetic bomb. I defuzed it and the Turkish police seemed impressed with my work and asked if I could take a look at their EOD teams and general EOD practice.

Everything was wrong, both in terms of lack of training and equipment and the general approach to EOD work. There was a horrifically macho quality to their attitude, and their methodology beggared belief: they would shoot at suspect bombs with pistols or chuck stones at them in hope of either initiating detonation or knocking them to pieces. I remember thinking at the scene of one incident that, as stone-throwers went, they were pretty good.

After a ten-day sojourn in what seemed like a lethal Wonderland with me unwittingly cast in the role of Alice, I returned to London, wrote a lengthy report with a wide range of recommendations, filed it, and forgot it.

Some weeks later the relevant authorities decided that, in the spirit of international co-operation, the Turkish police should be given assistance in bringing their EOD operators up to an acceptable standard. I was chosen to do the work and I asked Ken to accompany me. Not only were we old friends; Ken was both a very good explosives officer and a far better administrator than I. Since Roger's death we had become closer than ever before, a contrasting pair: me, tall and slim, Ken a broad-chested, blunt-speaking North Countryman.

'I see,' he said. 'I do all the donkey work and you get all the glamour.'

I feigned injured surprise. 'Come on. You know me better than that.'

He shoved his hands deeper into the pockets of the woollen cardigan he always wore. Finally: 'All right. I suppose somebody who knows what they're doing had better go.'

For the next six months we worked together in Turkey. Rarely had there been so much to do in so short a time; and rarely had there been better hosts: at every level of society the Turkish people proved themselves to be generous as well as joyous. From that date, longstanding friendships were formed; Ken and I looked forward to going back.

9

The Bomb-makers

My work at the Met brought me increasing satisfaction, especially when, in the wake of the London car bombs of March 1973, ten IRA terrorists were arrested, convicted in part on the strength of the evidence we had recovered from the vehicles and the defuzed car bombs. It was gratifying to know that I had not only taken out a threat but also helped to convict those responsible.

The war against the bombers had continued unabated, generally grim, usually depressing, only occasionally enlivened by encounters with alarm clocks with no hands and, in May 1974, a classic example of 'the Paddy Factor'.

The house was in Penystone Road, Maidenhead. An Irish gentleman owned the property but had let it to two other Irishmen while he attempted to sell it. The property was placed in the hands of a local estate agent, whose representative duly let himself in to examine the empty premises. His first surprise was that it showed signs of current occupancy, even though no one was there at the time of his visit. Then he discovered what looked like a large bag of catering sugar, about 12 pounds of the stuff. He telephoned the Maidenhead police to say that he'd stumbled across something which might be a bag filled with explosive. They arrived and checked the bag. No, they said, it wasn't explosive; it was just 12 pounds of catering sugar. However – they pointed to what seemed to be a 15-pound bag of cocoa powder – this *could* be explosive. At this point they called for an explosives officer and I was tasked to the scene.

By the time I arrived they'd completed the initial stages of a thoroughly professional job. Not only had they put a discreet security ring around the house by evacuating the residents on either side, a preliminary search of the rooms had yielded two detonators and a 9mm pistol. I went in to carry on the search while the police waited for the temporary occupant, or occupants, to return.

I began with the suspect explosive. It was cocoa. I rechecked the bag of sugar. It was sugar. I went upstairs and found almost 110 pounds of explosive and detonators. And then someone was knocking on the front door.

A policeman opened it and saw a young couple who could easily have been terrorists, except one of them then said: 'Excuse me, but we understand this house is for sale . . . ?'

No one was in a mood to take anyone at face value. They were slammed up against the wall, searched and then bundled off in a police car. They probably gave up house-hunting after that.

I went back to my search until someone else arrived downstairs: an Irishman who let himself in with a key. He walked along the hall and past the first room, at which point an armed policeman came out behind him while another jumped down the stairs and threw himself on to the floor with gun arm raised. At the end of the hall a third policeman also materialized with gun aimed. The terrorist lost control of his bladder. Wet and shaking, he was taken away.

I worked on into the night, searching as many corners and crevices of the house as possible.

It was dark when the other terrorist turned up. He was drunk and careless. He threw the back door open so hard that it slammed into the policeman who had been hiding behind it with gun cocked. The gun went off. The bullet smashed through the door and winged its way out across the driveway and into the kitchen of the neighbouring house. I was sitting next to a pile of highly sensitive nitroglycerine-based explosive; if the bullet had gone upwards instead of sideways the consequences could have been serious.

Like his compatriot, this second IRA terrorist was taken off to Maidenhead Police Station. He was very sober now, promising to be good and co-operative. The bombers were about as bright as they were brave: apart from the items we had found earlier, the police soon discovered all the evidence they needed to earn the pair very lengthy prison sentences. Though the terrorists had painstakingly hoovered up traces of their activities – dust, wrappings, tiny sections of cut wire – they hadn't thought to empty the vacuum cleaner's bag.

Another success story came on my forty-fourth birthday, 12 December 1975 – the day the Balcombe Street siege ended.

Four suspected IRA terrorists had opened fire when a policeman intercepted them near Marylebone Station. They ran into an apartment block in Balcombe Street, presumably thinking there was a way out through the back. There wasn't. They burst into a flat occupied by John and Sheila Matthews and took them hostage. Police ringed the building and waited.

After a week of headlines and high drama and painstaking negotiations, on the morning of 12 December Sheila Matthews was released. She was asked if the terrorists were in possession of explosives. She didn't know. They'd been carrying all kinds of things with them when they invaded the apartment, but she had seen them tie wire to the handle of one of the interior doors.

I was tasked to the scene and told about the possible booby-trap. It meant I'd have to enter the apartment before anyone else could. I arrived just before the siege ended and watched it on a closed circuit monitor in the control room. The monitor showed the front of the building. John Matthews came out first, moving carefully across his upper-storey balcony and then into the neighbouring apartment via its French windows. The terrorists followed. They had to go on their hands and knees to negotiate the route.

I moved in then. Initially I checked the hallway outside the flat, then went upstairs to the first-floor landing. I asked for the explosives sniffer dogs to be let loose; if one of them started barking I could call for a handler to interpret what the dog was signalling. The dogs went ahead of me. The handlers may well have wished to go with their dogs but in a situation like this, minimum risks must be taken.

The dogs didn't detect any explosive but one of them was so taken with a listening device which had been covertly stuck to the apartment's front door that he promptly ate it. I couldn't begin to imagine what kind of transmission the eavesdroppers were now picking up.

I went into the neighbouring apartment, clambered across their balcony and then the Matthews' to gain entry to the apartment. It was in a mess: six people had been living in one room for a week. They'd had food sent in during the closing stages of the siege and the styrofoam containers were everywhere.

There were no bombs and no booby-traps. The door handles had been connected to heavy pieces of furniture, not to prevent entry but to buy time for the terrorists to reach for their weapons and start shooting.

I checked the collection of guns left behind. There were two .357 Magnum revolvers loaded with .38 Special, two .38 revolvers and one 9mm Browning Short automatic. They'd also had a Sten gun which they'd either dropped or thrown away during the chase on 6 December, after they'd been intercepted in Rossmore Road. All that firepower and the four of them had run like hell from an unarmed Metropolitan Police inspector.

The four terrorists were identified as Martin Joseph O'Connell,

Edward Butler, Harry Duggan and Hugh Doherty. They later appeared at the Old Bailey on twenty-five separate charges including seven murders.

The victims were *Guinness Book of Records* co-author Ross McWhirter, murdered on 27 November 1975; Audrey Edgson, murdered as a result of an explosion at Walton's restaurant on 18 November; John Francis Batey, murdered as a result of an explosion at Scotts restaurant on 12 November; Gordon Hamilton-Fairey, murdered at Campden Hill Square on 23 October; Graham Ronald Tuck, murdered as a result of an explosion in Piccadilly on 9 October; and Robert Anthony Lloyd, murdered at the Hilton Hotel on 5 September. According to the charge sheet, their first victim was Roger Goad, murdered as a result of an explosion at 229 Kensington Church Street on 29 August.

The killers were sentenced to life imprisonment.

After our trip to Turkey in 1978, Ken and I had returned to a city which, having survived the violent onslaught of the IRA in the early seventies, was now experiencing a lull. Terrorist incidents still continued around the world: in February that year Red Brigade terrorists shot and killed a leading Italian judge; in March the Red Brigade kidnapped and subsequently killed Aldo Moro, five times Prime Minister of Italy; in June the President of North Yemen was killed by a parcel bomb; in July £1 million worth of damage was caused overnight by IRA incendiary attacks in Belfast; in August the IRA began bombing BAOR bases in Germany; in September the broadcaster Georgi Markov was killed in London by the Bulgarian secret police (a classic example of state terrorism); in November Basque terrorists shot dead a Spanish judge. Then, in December, IRA terrorists began the bombing of UK provincial cities, including Southampton, Bristol, Coventry and Manchester.

Within the space of a decade terrorism had become a grim fact of life in Europe.

In Britain, one man in particular was to bring terrorism into the eighties.

Patrick Joseph Magee was born on 29 May 1951 in Catholic West Belfast. At the age of three, Magee and his family moved to the UK mainland and settled in Norwich where he was brought up as an English child with an English education.

In 1966, Magee left school and worked as a labourer. He also tried his hand at shop-breaking but was caught and placed on two years' probation.

In 1969, he moved back to Belfast with his family and he was seen in the company of a known Provisional. Two years later, the family returned to England but Magee stayed on. In 1972, at the age of twenty-one, he became the Youth Organizer for the Provisional IRA and was subsequently interned for two years at the Long Kesh Internment Centre. Here, between 1973 and 1975, he found himself in the company of hardened IRA men who quickly realized his potential as a terrorist: Patrick Joseph Magee could easily pass as an Englishman. On his release from Long Kesh he visited two Libyan terrorist training centres to further refine the bomb-making skills he had learned during internment.

In August 1977, in advance of the Queen's visit to Coleraine University, Northern Ireland, a search of the grounds uncovered devices featuring a previously unused type of electronic long-delay timer. The bombs were timed to explode twelve days later when the Queen was actually on the campus.

It was the first known operational use of long-delay timers.

Further discoveries of devices with long-delay timers were made in Germany and mainland UK including a dozen hidden under floorboards at a flat in Greenwich in January 1979. Forensic evidence concluded that this had been a safe house for an IRA bombing team.

In June 1979 six letter bombs were defuzed and nine exploded in the Birmingham postal system. Each device contained an electronic arming circuit similar to the long-delay timers. They had been ssembled in Ireland, brought over and posted in Birmingham. After forensic evaluation of the defuzed devices, a warrant was issued for Magee's arrest.

Magee fled to Holland but, in September 1980, after being alerted by their British counterparts, the Dutch police arrested him. Three months later a Dutch court refused to extradite him to Britain, released him, and he returned to Ireland.

Little was known of his whereabouts until 15 September 1984 when, using a false name and address, Magee checked in to the Grand Hotel, Brighton. He made an advance cash payment of £180 for a three-night stay. He was allocated Room 629, five floors directly above that which Margaret Thatcher would occupy a few weeks later for the annual Conservative Party Conference.

On the night of 17 September 1984 Magee hid a long-delay electronically timed device containing around 11 kilograms of high explosive behind a bath panel in Room 629. He left the Grand Hotel the following day and, for the next three weeks, other guests continued to use the room and its ensuite bathroom.

On 8 October the Conservative Party Conference opened. The Grand Hotel was fully booked with high-ranking party officials including the Prime Minister and several Cabinet Ministers.

Magee's bomb exploded at 2.54 a.m. on Friday 12 October. It blew apart the bath, tore down the walls and toppled the huge chimney stack from the roof above, sending it crashing down through the floors to the basement below. Five prominent members of the Conservative Party were killed and thirty injured, some permanently disabled.

I drove to Brighton the day after the bombing. The elegant façade of the Grand Hotel was riven apart, its central section a huge tumble of rubble. Damage and death had been caused not so much by the bomb's power as its position. The collapse of the hotel's central flooring area was due entirely to the weight of the chimney crashing through from the roof to ground level.

Returning to London, I undertook a survey of metropolitan

buildings likely to be used by public figures. What emerged was
that buildings are designed to cope with downward, not upward,
thrusts. You can put tremendous weights on some floors, but apply
a tenth of that force in an upward direction and they will break.
When that happens, they come crashing down along with their
walls. Catastrophic weakening of the structure accompanied by the
sudden impact of plunging masonry will not reduce an entire building to rubble but it can – as in the case of the Grand Hotel – result
in severe localized floor-by-floor damage.

Aware now of the threat implicit in building design, particularly
that of some older structures, I was dismayed by the evidence of
my survey. Unfortunately, identifying a risk is one thing, dealing
with it, quite another. To even attempt to rectify design flaws in
some of the buildings surveyed would have cost millions, and most
likely have destroyed their character as a result.

As for discreetly advising, for instance, that a particular hotel
should not be used for a Royal function, that was likewise out of
the question: word would gradually get out, facts be distorted and
rumours amplified, and finally the hotel would be deserted by its
clientele and face financial ruin through no fault of its own.

The survey was filed after completion. We had acquired a great
deal of knowledge but would never have the wherewithal to make
much use of it.

Shortly after the Brighton bombing the IRA issued a statement
admitting responsibility and adding: 'Today we were unlucky. But
remember – we only have to be lucky once.'

Sussex police set about the mammoth task of tracing all guests
in the preceding month. They managed to eliminate 800 people in
fifty countries including two sets of American tourists and an Indian
visitor from Bombay. Eventually they were left with the signatory
to the Room 629 registration card of 15 September.

In the meantime, 3,798 dustbins containing evidence from the
explosion together with a further 46,000 pounds of debris were
loaded on to trucks and delivered to the Forensic Explosives Lab

oratory. Forensic analysis subsequently confirmed that the device had featured components consistent with a long-delay timer as well as two PP9 batteries – needed to power long-delay timers.

Analysis of the Grand Hotel registration card revealed prints from a left little finger and a right palm. In January 1985 a crossmatch was made with the prints taken from Patrick Joseph Magee by the Norwich police in 1966. The false name was also identified: Magee had signed himself in under the name of a friend – a known Provisional – who could not possibly have signed the register as he was serving a life sentence for his role in the London car bomb attacks of March 1973.

Anti-terrorist chiefs decided not to go public with their knowledge of Magee's involvement. Instead they waited for him to return to the mainland. Their patience was rewarded less than six months later when, on 15 June 1985, Magee checked in to London's Rubens Hotel. He used a different false name to sign the registration card for Room 112, which faced on to the Queen's Picture Gallery in Buckingham Palace. He set a long-delay timer to initiate a 3½-pound bomb on 29 July and then concealed the device behind a fitted bedside cabinet. He left the Rubens Hotel the following day for a safe house in Scotland – the headquarters of what was intended to be the most vicious IRA bombing campaign Britain had ever seen.

The campaign targeted London as well as twelve British seaside resorts.

Magee joined the other members of his terrorist group at their flat in Langside Road, Glasgow. On 22 June Peter Sherry, credited by security sources with at least fifteen murders, left his home in Dungannon, Northern Ireland and travelled to the Scottish port of Stranraer. He did not realize he was under twenty-four hour surveillance by the Royal Ulster Constabulary.

At 7.40 p.m. on 22 June detectives burst into the Glasgow apartment and arrested the five occupants: Patrick Magee, Peter Sherry, Gerald McDonnell, Ella O'Dwyer and Martina Anderson. They found a number of fake passports, handguns and wigs, £20,000 in cash and a log setting out the schedule for the summer bombing campaign: sixteen bombs were intended to explode in daily succession in London and the twelve seaside resorts. According to the schedule, one of the bombs was already in place in Room 112 of the Rubens Hotel, London.

Detailed information about the bomb and its location was sent through to us on the morning of 23 June. One of my colleagues was immediately tasked to the scene. Only when I arrived for the start of my duty shift did I learn what was happening: an Expo was at the hotel and undertaking the search procedure.

This was very unusual; Explosives Officers do not normally get called in until after a search has been completed and a find made. On this occasion, however, the detailed information received from Scotland indicated that this was a high-risk operation: a bomb was in Room 112 and was very likely to be booby-trapped.

My duty shift was to follow on from the Expo at the Rubens, so I hastened to the hotel. The device had at last been located by the Expo's driver. It had been so securely hidden that had there not been a ninety-nine per cent certainty of its existence, it could well have evaded detection.

My colleague and I stared at the package. It had been hidden in the void at the base of the bedside cabinet. X-rays revealed the presence of two anti-handler mechanisms: a mercury-tilt switch and a micro-switch. The long-delay timer had been set, the timer to arm the bomb had closed and the arming obviously completed some time ago. If the device had been moved even a fraction of an inch, it would have exploded. Accordingly, we decided to use the disrupter.

We positioned it with great care, moving as much furniture out of the way as possible to permit the greatest accuracy of aim. We ran the firing cable out of the window, down on to Buckingham Palace Road below, and along to a shop doorway where the four of us gathered together in a tight huddle: my colleague and myself and our two police drivers.

The firing cable was connected to a device which generates an electric current to fire the disrupter. My colleague grinned at me. 'Go on. You do it.'

I shook my head. 'Thanks, but your driver found the bomb. He should have the honour of pressing the button.'

'Whoa,' said the driver. 'Not me.'

'Look,' I said. 'How often does a police constable have the chance to blow up a London hotel and not get blamed for it?'

He considered for only a moment. 'Ah well, when you put it like that.' And he fired the disrupter.

The Rubens did not blow up. The disrupter worked perfectly, blasting the device's internal circuitry to smithereens. We went back into Room 112 to survey the various fragments and pieces of explosive that had erupted outwards under the force of the ultra-high-velocity water jet. We were looking at the last bomb of the man who tried to kill the British Prime Minister.

On 10 June 1986 Peter Sherry, aged thirty, Gerald McDonnell, thirty-five, Ella O'Dwyer, twenty-six, and Martina Anderson, twenty-three, were sentenced to life imprisonment for their conspiracy to cause explosions in the summer holiday season of 1985.

Patrick Joseph Magee, thirty-five, was convicted of the murders of the five victims of the Grand Hotel bombing and of conspiring to cause explosions in the summer campaign. He was given eight life sentences and the judge recommended he should serve not less than thirty-five years. If Magee serves the minimum term, he will be released when he is seventy years old. The year will be 2021.

10

Terror from the Middle East

The attempted bombing of an El Al flight by Nezar Nawaf Mansour Hindawi was the first example of State terrorism to be proved in a UK Court. A Jordanian national, Hindawi was born in 1954. Though his mother and sisters continued to live in Jordan, Hindawi's father and one of his brothers took up permanent residence in the UK. Hindawi came to England in 1980 to visit his brother. He enrolled on a succession of English language courses and became the London correspondent for a number of Arab journals. In December 1980 he married a Polish national also living in London; the couple separated not long afterwards.

In late 1984 Hindawi was introduced by a mutual friend to thirty-year-old Ann Murphy. Dublin-born and bred, she arrived in London in October of that year and found work as a hotel chambermaid. Hindawi left London at Christmas 1984 and reappeared at Murphy's staff quarters two months later, when she informed him she had recently had a miscarriage. Hindawi proposed to her, saying he was divorcing his wife. Bizarrely, he also asked if she could put him in touch with the Provisional IRA for the purposes of 'a journalistic interview'. Murphy had no idea what he was talking about and Hindawi vanished again, reappearing briefly before leaving for an undisclosed overseas destination in November. This latest departure occurred shortly after Murphy revealed that she was pregnant again.

On 7 April 1986 Hindawi suddenly materialized on Murphy's doorstep. He had missed her, he said, and to make up for his behaviour would like to take her on a holiday to Israel where they would be married. He gave her the telephone and room number of his London hotel.

On 14 April Hindawi told her they would have to travel separately; she could go direct but he had first to go to Jordan on a ticket prepurchased by his employer. He would meet her a few hours after her arrival in Tel Aviv. Ann Murphy did not relish the prospect of travelling alone but Hindawi told her that if she didn't agree then she needn't bother going at all. She had to comply.

On 16 April Hindawi presented Murphy with a large holdall, 'a bag with wheels' as he described it. It would, he said, be far better for her than her existing suitcases. They talked for a while about the next day's travel arrangements, during which time Hindawi kept fiddling with a pocket calculator. He then packed her clothes – and the calculator – into the holdall and left.

At 7.20 a.m. on Thursday 17 April 1986 Hindawi returned in a taxi and the couple then travelled to Heathrow Airport. Although he was supposed to be flying to Jordan at the same time, his absence of luggage aroused no suspicion in Ann Murphy's mind. Unused to international travel and very much in love with her husband-to-be, Murphy had no idea of Hindawi's private plans for her, her unborn child, and the other 374 passengers and crew of the El Al flight to Tel Aviv.

En route to Heathrow Hindawi opened Murphy's luggage and removed the calculator. He inserted a battery, then returned the calculator to the holdall, this time delving deep to ensure it was placed at the bottom of the holdall. Murphy did not ask why he was so preoccupied with the calculator.

Hindawi kissed her goodbye at the departure terminal; in only a few hours, he said, they would meet again in Tel Aviv. She mustn't worry about anything.

Murphy made her way to Gate 23 for the El Al flight. An airline security officer noticed the holdall and decided to subject it to a thorough search. Its contents were removed in her presence, including the pocket calculator. An El Al security woman did a calculation and it functioned normally. The bag was twice placed in a fluoroscope and X-rayed but gave no cause for concern.

However, when one of the security staff picked up the holdall with the intention of repacking Murphy's belongings, it occurred to him that for an empty piece of airline baggage it was unexpectedly heavy, so it was taken to a nearby office and stripped down. After removing its interior cardboard base, security staff discovered a flat blue plastic package measuring 16 inches by 9 inches by ⅛ inch, shaped to the contours of the bag. It was wrapped up with buff-coloured parcel tape and secured in place with double-sided adhesive tape.

I arrived at the evacuated terminal at 10.10 a.m. and was briefed by an inspector from the Heathrow Airport police. Until the briefing, all I knew was that El Al had found what they thought might be a bomb in a passenger's luggage. The Inspector explained that the passenger had been through British Airways security before being allowed to enter the transit lounge, but that El Al ran their own security and were not content to depend on anyone else. He escorted me to the office, pointed out the holdall and left me to it. The blue plastic package had been removed and a corner torn off to reveal a section of orange-coloured substance resembling Semtex. Clearly this was the main charge of a bomb.

I X-rayed it in order to locate the initiator but found nothing; X-rayed it again: nothing. Gingerly I unwrapped the package, set it down on the table and tried again: still nothing. All I was looking at was 3 pounds 4 ounces of high explosive – a bare charge.

Security staff said they'd already subjected the passenger's belongings to a rigorous inspection and found nothing, so the initiator had to be somewhere inside the holdall. But where? Concealed in the holdall's tubular frame? Hidden in the wheels?

The X-ray machine went into action again, producing one image after another of – nothing. I scanned the holdall from every conceivable angle, examined every millimetre of its construction, turned it inside out and upside down and still ... nothing. It did not make sense.

Nobody would be stupid enough to attempt to transport bare explosive to Israel on board an El Al flight. Someone might attempt to get a bomb aboard, but not bare explosive; there were easier ways of getting HE across international borders than risking it on an airline with a reputation for the tightest security.

I checked my watch: 11.13 a.m. I had spent an hour on the main charge and the holdall. There had to be a mechanism to initiate detonation. If it wasn't in this room then it had to be amongst the passenger's belongings which security staff had previously removed at the search table by Gate 23.

I went and stared at the jumble of things spread out over the length of the search table. All this stuff had been checked by the ultra-zealous El Al security, so the initiator must have been very well hidden indeed. There was nothing else for it: I would have to work methodically from one end of the table to the other.

Perfumes, pots of cream, sandals, shoes, hairdryer, clothes – it was like trying to analyse the individual items of a jumble sale. I X-rayed everything, opened the perfume bottles, stuck my fingers in the pots of cream, took images of the sandals because I knew there'd been an earlier case of an initiator being built into the heel of a shoe. I found nothing.

Then I came across an old brass boot, an ornament 5 inches long by 2½ inches high. This could be it, I thought. The hollow boot could provide a good hiding place for a bomb and the metal casing would act as a barrier to X-ray inspection.

My X-ray machine was on the verge of smoking. I aimed it at

the boot and punched in the maximum number of pulses but the brass was too thick for the X-rays to penetrate. I moved the machine closer to the boot and tried again but I still got only an outline of the ornament. Once more, even closer. Finally I got through and found the old brass boot was . . . an old brass boot. (I later discovered it had been a wedding present to Ann Murphy and her prospective husband.)

It was 11.35 a.m. and I had totally knackered the X-ray machine: you're supposed to allow something like five minutes for the machine to cool after intensive activity but I didn't know if I *had* five minutes – better to ruin an X-ray tube than sit around waiting and be blown to pieces by a bomb.

I picked up the calculator. Security staff had already checked it. It functioned normally. It was what it appeared to be – except that when I turned it over and examined the retaining screws at the back, they seemed somehow . . . shiny, as if they were under a layer of clear glue. I paused and wondered about that, then carefully prised apart the front and back of the calculator and saw a piece of white tape inside. That was wrong too. Calculators do not normally contain white tape.

I returned to the screws but was unable to remove them because they had been cemented into place with an epoxy resin. Instead, I used wire-cutters to split open the plastic casing around the screws and levered the thing wide open. And there it was: a bomb.

The interior contained two small packages, one wrapped in white tape, the other in brown. I wasn't an authority on calculators but I knew that these items shouldn't be there. I took a photograph of the device and put the camera outside the room. If anything went wrong, at least the forensic experts would have something to go on. I slit open the brown package and discovered 1½ ounces of Semtex with a detonator embedded in it. I separated the two and then realized that if I disconnected the timer unit from the battery I would never know when this thing was set to go off – it was functioning on an integrated circuit (often known as a chip timer), not a mechanical timer. A scientist could say that this particular chip timer was designed to run for a certain number of hours, but he could not say when it had been set; which meant that if a number of people had been handling the bomb, there would be no evidence to suggest who had armed it.

Accordingly I disconnected the detonator without disconnecting the battery from the timer circuit and then replaced the detonator with a tiny device called an Ignitor Safety Fuze Electric (a detonator without detonating composition). I placed it back on the table and informed security and officers from the Met's Anti-Terrorist Branch of what I had done.

At 1.04 p.m. the igniter went off with a crack and a puff of smoke. Had the El Al jet departed on schedule, it would have been 800 miles away, high above southern Europe. It was five hours since Hindawi had opened the calculator in the taxi to Heathrow – five hours since he had armed the bomb.

After kissing Ann Murphy goodbye, Hindawi had returned to his own hotel, collected his luggage, then headed for the Royal Garden Hotel, Kensington. He was due to fly to Syria at 2 p.m., travelling to Heathrow on a Syrian Arab Airlines crew bus. However, when the bus arrived he was handed a sealed letter by a member of the crew and instructed to go instead to 8 Belgrave Square: the Syrian Arab Embassy.

At the embassy Hindawi presented his letter and was warmly welcomed by a Syrian diplomat who then introduced him to three others, including a Dr Haydar, described as 'the Ambassador'. In Hindawi's presence, the Ambassador made a call to Damascus, and then told Hindawi that certain persons in Damascus were 'very pleased' with him. According to Hindawi's later statement, Dr Haydar said it had been decided to keep him in hiding for a few days; he would be taken to a safe place.

Hindawi was driven to a house in Stonor Road, West Kensington, which had been let to one of the diplomats on 7 August 1985, although it was not listed as his official residence. There Hindawi's hair was cut and dyed. At 5 a.m. the following day, Friday 18 April, Hindawi was woken by two of the diplomats and told he was being taken back to the Syrian Arab Embassy. Something about the situation made Hindawi suddenly apprehensive; on the pavement outside the house he began arguing, was grabbed by one of the men, broke free and ran off down the road, shouting at the top of his voice. The two diplomats jumped into their car and sped off without pursuing him.

Hindawi roamed the streets for some time and then checked into the London Visitor's Hotel. But the Metropolitan Police had obtained vital evidence from Ann Murphy and circulated Hindawi's picture the previous day. As Hindawi was registering at the hotel he was recognized and the police summoned.

In the wake of Hindawi's arrest, the Stonor Road address was searched by police and a quantity of cut hair found in a wastepaper bin. It matched Hindawi's. Hindawi also provided police with an accurate sketch map of the interior of the Syrian Arab Embassy and descriptions of the Ambassador and his three colleagues.

As police now had in custody a man who had planned to kill the woman who loved him, her unborn child, and 374 other men, women and children, the Syrian Ambassador and his staff were asked to cooperate with the criminal investigation enquiries in progress. The request was refused. Within hours Britain broke off diplomatic relations with Syria; the Ambassador and all his staff were summarily expelled.

In October 1986 Nezar Nawaf Mansour Hindawi appeared at the Old Bailey.

The evidence was damning: forensic scientists had indeed been able to work back from the time my little ISFE went off at 1.04 p.m. to show that the chip timer was designed to set off a detonator after a five-hour delay. Hindawi had been seen handling the calculator at 8.04 a.m. by both the taxi driver and Ann Murphy.

In his summing up Mr Justice Mars-Jones said: 'A more callous and cruel deception, and a more horrendous massacre, would be hard to imagine.' I watched as Hindawi was sentenced. He smiled broadly, saluted the Court and was led from the dock.

None of us could understand his reaction. But then, none of us knew that Hindawi hadn't understood the Judge. It was only when Defence Counsel went down to see his client in the holding cell that Hindawi's misapprehension was corrected. He thought he had been sentenced to 'four to five years', hence his jubilant face in Court. In fact he'd been given forty-five years – the longest prison sentence ever handed out by a UK Court. Upon learning the truth Hindawi promptly collapsed.

Though diplomatic privilege precluded the arrest of Dr Haydar and the other three diplomats, Syrian complicity in a mass murder conspiracy was never in doubt.

The Hindawi case also brought to our attention a new kind of aircraft bomb, one where the main charge was separate from the initiating system.

Hindawi must have known that black-and-white X-rays have great difficulty in identifying hidden explosive – it looks like a grey mass, and when positioned at the bottom of a case tends to merge into its structure. All the things which security people would look out for – batteries, detonator outline, wiring – were not present but hidden inside a separate and mundane item of equipment which they assumed couldn't possibly be a bomb since you can't pack enough HE to blow up an aircraft into something as small as a pocket calculator.

The calculator would have blown up first, triggering sympathetic detonation of the main charge a millisecond later. It made the ideal initiating system because you expect to find batteries and electric circuitry in such equipment.

In the wake of the Heathrow incident I made a mock-up of Hindawi's bomb. There had been two chips instead of one, the first as standard equipment to work the calculator, the second incorporated by the bomb-maker to operate the timer. He had also placed the small quantity of Semtex and a detonator on top of the circuit board. When I X-rayed my mock-up I couldn't easily discern the detonator, even though I knew where it was. As for the presence of two chips, I very much doubt if anyone other than the designer could have said how many chips should have been in that calculator. Hindawi's bomb had been specifically designed to defeat X-ray examination and, in that respect, was extremely successful.

I was pleased with the outcome of the affair. Until then, no one had thought to disconnect a detonator and connect in its place something which would prove the time of the intended explosion. I was also relieved that I had not ignored a stubborn intuition which kept insisting that, despite the lack of evidence, despite the time expended on the main charge, the holdall, and all its contents, up to and including the old brass boot, there *had* to be an initiator somewhere; that this was not just a cache of bare explosive.

The Hindawi affair took me back to my days at Hounslow and our DIY depressurization chamber. Prior to that time bombs on aircraft were very crude and rarely associated with terrorism; an explosion was more likely to be caused by someone sending his wife off with a suitcase full of dynamite in order to claim the insurance.

But then Middle Eastern terrorists began to emerge, and they incorporated barometric switches into the bomb timing mechanism, knowing that it was futile to depend on timers alone: a plane could be delayed for hours on the ground with passengers still stuck in the departure lounge; you needed to ensure that the timer didn't begin to function until the barometric switch had detected the change of pressure when the aircraft became airborne. To each counter-terrorism tactic, Arab terrorists responded with increasing sophistication; soon, explosive was being built into the linings of suitcases and metallic components hidden in the metal framework.

Until after the Lockerbie disaster in December 1988 passengers were still allowed to transport battery-powered objects in luggage destined for an aircraft's hold. You expected to find batteries in radios, calculators, or children's toys. But those batteries could simultaneously be powering something else, as in Nezar Hindawi's calculator.

Not until 1989 was anything done to prevent all passengers on all airlines from carrying batteries in luggage sent to an aircraft's hold. Some airlines banned them, others did not. Lockerbie, and the alleged radio bomb aboard the Pan Am jumbo, was to change all that, but the Hindawi incident had already been well-documented two and a half years earlier; the lack of reaction can only be attributed to complacency.

Despite all today's precautions – including the colour differential X-ray system – I still think Lockerbie could happen again. We have improved our defences against the terrorists but it is always a case of they lead, we follow; they act, we respond.

For instance in 1987, the year after Hindawi's bomb attempt was frustrated, an Arab was carrying two bottles of wine through Frankfurt Airport. An alert Customs officer stopped the man for questioning, was dissatisfied with the answers he received, detained the Arab, and sent the bottles away for forensic examination.

It was a wise move. Instead of wine, the factory-sealed bottles were filled with methyl nitrate, an extremely dangerous liquid high explosive. Similar to nitroglycerine and normally colourless, methyl nitrate can be dyed to resemble anything you want – whisky, rum, sherry or wine. In a suitcase or a bag it is unlikely to provoke suspicion even when X-rayed; in weight and appearance it is just a bottle of Duty Free, not a container filled with liquid explosive.

Methyl nitrate is exceptionally sensitive to a detonating shock-wave, even more so than liquid nitroglycerine, so the proximity of main charge to detonator is far less crucial than it was in the El Al bomb, when Hindawi had to delve deep into Ann Murphy's holdall when positioning the calculator (if he'd left it at the top of the bag, the detonating charge would have been separated from the main charge by layers of clothing, and would have been unlikely to set off the main charge.) But if Hindawi had placed a bottle of methyl

nitrate in the holdall, it would not have mattered where the calculator was placed: regardless of anything between them, the main
charge would have gone off.

It is not clear if methyl nitrate is being used by terrorists for
bombs in aircraft; it may well be that the banning of batteries in
passenger luggage and the use of colour differential X-ray is causing the bombers to rethink their tactics. However, those arrested
for the bombing of a Korean jet shortly before the Seoul Olympics
claimed to have used liquid explosive.

Although an airline can be run with virtually a hundred per cent
security, it is unlikely that many passengers would wish to travel
on it. No matter what people say, no matter how loud the clarion
call for greater safety, an airline which banned all electrical goods,
which insisted on a five-hour check-in, and which strip-searched
every passenger, would rapidly go out of business. People do not
wish to endure such massive inconvenience because, deep down,
they do not think anything will happen to them. Death is something which only happens to others.

The trouble with embassies, I thought, is that diplomatic immunity
only goes so far. On 7 May 1980 Ken and I were standing in the
wreckage of the Telex Room of the Iranian Embassy. I'd just
managed to disentangle myself from a corpse and a Russian RGL
5 hand grenade.

Until then I had given little thought to the kind of life enjoyed
by foreign embassy staff. Stories of diplomats owing thousands of
pounds in unpaid parking tickets or of diplomats' wives escaping
prosecution for shop-lifting had left jaundiced Londoners with the
distinct feeling that there was one law for the diplomats and another
for everyone else. There were circumstances, however, where
diplomatic immunity didn't apply: diplomats couldn't say to a
bomb, 'Excuse me, I'm on embassy premises.'

The Iranian Embassy siege began on 30 April when, in the
name of a factional extremist cause, armed terrorists burst into the

uilding and took many of the staff hostage. Negotiations proved
ruitless; after the murder of two hostages the SAS stormed the
mbassy on 5 May and killed five of the six gunmen. The operation
vas watched by millions of TV viewers worldwide.

Clear-up work began on 6 May; the Met's Explosives Office was
alled in to declare the building safe from explosives. In the wake
f the siege and its violent conclusion the place was littered with
ne remains of grenades and small arms ammunition. Fire damage
vas extensive; you only had to look at the once-proud façade of
he Prince's Gate building to know that it had been a war zone.

Two Expos were tasked because of the magnitude of the job.
We started on the ground floor and then carefully worked upwards,
loor by floor, dealing with unsafe items as we found them, leaving
others which we considered to be safe where they were, their
xistence signalled by little markers.

There had been a tremendous battle followed by a fire in the
ecretary's room on the first floor. In amongst the scattering of
istols and grenades, fired ammunition and the remains of stun
grenades, lay the body of one of the terrorists. There was also a
ase containing sunglasses, film cassette, lighter, razor, and tube of
Chapstick. I looked at this, then at the body, sprawled out with a
9mm pistol at its side. I'd never have thought a hardened terrorist
vould worry about something as mundane as chapped lips.

The back room contained the body of a second terrorist, badly
urned by the fire caused when stun grenades set light to the
urtains. Here, as everywhere else, the stench of smoke was over-
vhelming; charred wood and blackened plasterwork crumbled at
he slightest touch.

The second floor wasn't immediately accessible because the stair-
ase had almost burned away. A surveyor told us we couldn't go
here until the floor had been shored up but we got tired of waiting
nd found a ladder. Three bodies were in the Telex Room; they'd
ave to be moved but there was no way of telling what might be
eneath them. They may have been shot by the SAS; then again,

one of them might have been a hostage shot by the gunmen and left to lie on the floor with a booby-trap to catch the unwary.

It was then that I slipped my hand under one of the bodies and touched the grenade. We had already found one RGD 5 behind the door. I thought quickly: it is not unusual in war time to leave a corpse lying on a grenade from which the pin has been removed; lift the body and the grenade goes off. The only thing to do if you hear the igniter strike is to drop the corpse back on to the grenade and let it shield you from the blast.

Ken stayed well back; no point in two of us being caught out. I kept my fingers clamped on the grenade and cautiously moved it clear. It was safe. The pin had not been pulled. We both breathed easily again.

In April 1984 I found myself back on embassy premises, this time after the murder of Woman Police Constable Yvonne Fletcher. She had been trying to control an angry crowd of demonstrators gathered outside the Peoples' Bureau of the Socialist Peoples' Libyan Arab Jamahiriya when she was killed by gunfire from a first-floor window.

It was an act of vicious callousness and the Libyans refused to hand the killer over to the authorities. As a result the embassy was surrounded by police and no one allowed in or out.

After prolonged negotiations the siege ended on 29 April. The Libyans were forced to quit both the building and the country. Their departure provoked a public uproar; a defenceless young policewoman had been shot down in the line of duty and the Libyans couldn't have cared less. A memorial fund was launched under the chairmanship of film director Michael Winner; today a plaque marking the place where Yvonne Fletcher died says everything that needs to be said about the obscenity of State-sponsored terrorism.

I was tasked to 5 St James's Square on 30 April. Originally team from the Royal Engineers was going in to search the place but they were so hampered by army regulations that five hours fter arriving at the scene they still hadn't entered the building.

I watched and inwardly fretted as the clock ticked on from 1.40 a.m., when the RE team arrived, to 4.40 p.m., by which time he light was fading fast and they had only managed to open the ack door and remove, one at a time, more than sixty sacks of ubbish from an inner passageway. I decided to go in by myself hen.

The negotiation period prior to the Libyans' departure had given hem plenty of time to do as they wished to the building, so we could not rule out the possibility of a bomb somewhere inside – if t exploded and killed a lot of people, the Libyans would doubtless claim it was all our fault.

A possible source of risk was the burglar alarm system, triggered by sensors fitted to the concertina-style metal window grilles. If that was linked to a bomb, then breaking in could cause an explosion. Fortunately we had tracked down the firm who had installed the system and I had obtained some sample sensors the day before the siege ended. I had found a way to neutralize them without activating the alarm.

I decided to go in through the kitchen at the back of the building. I used a glass-cutter on the window, knocked out the sensor, waited while a Public Works team cut through the grille, then clambered in. The place was in darkness; the Libyans had closed all the curtains as well as the grilles. The room stank of cheap aftershave. I edged through the gloom, using my torch to look for trip wires and other booby traps, to where I knew the burglar alarm control panel was sited. I trod carefully on the marble edge of the flooring, determined to avoid walking on the carpet in case there were hidden pressure switches. When I finally reached the control panel I felt rather silly: the bloody thing had never been switched on.

A thorough search of the building showed it was free of IEDs and booby-traps. It also showed how determined the Libyans had been to remove or destroy as much material as possible: the place looked as though it had been vandalized from top to bottom. Every room was in chaos, filled with upturned filing cabinets and tipped-over furniture.

I paused by the first-floor window overlooking St James's Square and stared down at the place where WPC Yvonne Fletcher had died. Then I bent down to examine the floor beneath the central heating radiator and found a spent 9mm cartridge. The Libyans hadn't been as thorough as they'd thought.

11

The Wimpy Bar

The Downing Street mortar attack in 1991 was one of the most
brilliant terrorist operations ever carried out on the UK mainland.
Though I have no sympathy with terrorism's aims and objectives,
it has to be said that those who masterminded and executed the
attack did so with a precision of which the military would have
been proud.

It was, in terrorist terms, both a tactical achievement (in that
they got so close to the target, and operated under the very eyes
of armed police) and a propaganda and psychological victory, for
the attack served to remind everyone of the terrorists' determination and of the vulnerability of even the Prime Minister and his
Cabinet to an attack in the very heart of London.

It did not, however, alter the fact that true and enduring achievement belongs not to the terrorists but to ordinary people in Northern Ireland and mainland Britain and in every country in the world
where there is a determination not to give in. As for the victory,
that also belongs to ordinary people – particularly to those who,
in sacrificing their own lives so that others may live, become the
most special people of all.

Monday 26 October 1981 was a typical autumn day in the capital,

brisk, fresh, and sunlit. The events of that day began shortly before
I arrived on duty, with a radio message to PC David Wallace and
PC Damian Manning as they patrolled 'C' Division in their area
car. They had received a message from Control at 3.05 p.m. saying,
'Bomb threat at the Wimpy Bar between Debenhams and Bourne
and Hollingsworth, Oxford Street, W.1.'

Using the car's two-tone horns, they made a high-speed dash to
the scene, arriving within a few minutes of receiving the message.
They alerted the manager to the threat and began a search of the
ground-floor dining area, moving quickly but without unnecessary
dramatics: Oxford Street was, as ever, thronged with shoppers and
tourists and the Wimpy Bar was still busy in mid-afternoon. It was
important not to provoke an uncontrolled rush to the exit.

The preliminary search yielded nothing, and PC Wallace
returned to the car to talk to Control. He was told that a second
message had just been received which not only confirmed the first
but indicated that the bomb had been placed downstairs in the
basement area toilets.

Wallace, Manning and the manager went to investigate; while
Wallace and the manager checked the ladies' toilets, Manning
entered the gents and discovered what he later described as 'a
parcel and a box' underneath the twin sinks. By Manning's estimate
at the time, the parcel had rounded edges and was 9 inches by
6 inches by 1½ inches. It was wrapped in brown sticky tape about
2 inches wide and was approximately 2 to 3 inches from the box.
The box reminded Manning of 'a school pencil box', although it
was smaller: about 5 inches by 3 inches by 1½ inches.

PC Wallace came in to confirm the presence of the packages
and then the two officers and the manager evacuated everyone
from the premises. Wallace asked Control to send an explosives
officer to the scene.

I arrived at the Bungalow at about 3.40 p.m., twenty minutes
before the start of my shift. This was standard Expo practice; you
needed time to familiarize yourself with the events of the day, read

incoming messages and check your equipment. However, it rapidly became clear that time was in very short supply. The Bungalow was at the centre of a major alert: according to Control, an anonymous telephone call had been received by the Reuters News Agency warning that the IRA had planted *three* bombs in Oxford Street, one in Bourne and Hollingsworth, one in Debenhams, and one in the Wimpy Bar at 142–144 Oxford Street.

I was further told that a search of the three locations had been made and two outwardly identical suspect explosive devices located, one in the Wimpy Bar and the other in Debenhams. The duty Expo had been tasked to the Wimpy Bar at 3.35 p.m., just a few minutes before I had arrived at the Bungalow. Even while this briefing was going on, events in Oxford Street were rapidly progressing.

Police officers were combing Bourne and Hollingsworth as customers emptied out on to the pavement, joining the hundreds of others continuing to emerge from surrounding shops and stores. Like a bewildered army in colourful and uncomprehending disarray, the crowds were marshalled away to safety beyond the cordons. All around, traffic came to a standstill as central London plunged into a noisy paralysis of sirens and car horns, as more Metropolitan Police vehicles moved in to secure both ends of the no-go area.

Meanwhile, at the Wimpy Bar, the Expo had arrived. He was briefed by PCs Wallace and Manning and helped into his flak jacket. He then went into the empty premises and disappeared into the basement. The two police officers waited outside, standing now in the middle of the wide, deserted thoroughfare. In the space of less than thirty minutes, a large section of one of the most famous streets in the world had been stilled. Only the squawk and static of police radios and emergency vehicles broke the silence. The unreality of it all made each second tick by with aching slowness. And then the explosion came.

Muffled rather than loud, distant rather than near, the sound

registered only for an instant before the Wimpy Bar's frontage
dissolved in a cloud of grey-brown smoke. Glass and wood spewed
outwards in a whirling storm and a section of concrete pavement
disintegrated as it hurtled across Oxford Street. The smoke blos-
somed and billowed, and a dense dark column climbed skywards
even as the last pieces of debris thudded and tinkled on to the
asphalt.

News of the blast came while I was still being briefed. Even
before the news came through I had decided that we had a serious
situation on our hands because the *exact* location of the bomb had
been given. Experience told me that the IRA were never that
helpful, never that specific. It was as though they were encouraging
an Expo to get to the scene and daring him to deal with the device.
Whatever had been placed there had to be very nasty indeed, and
the seemingly identical Debenhams device very likely posed a
similar threat.

As for the Expo, no one appeared to know whether he was alive
or dead, whether he had been injured or had been well away from
the bomb when it went off. I grabbed my kit and told the Controller
I was going to the Wimpy Bar and then on to Debenhams. All of
us, not just me, had to know what had happened in that basement.

I couldn't find anyone who had actually been into the basement
after the explosion. Though it was possible the police at the other
end of the street knew more, those I met at my arrival point could
only say that yes, an explosives officer had entered the premises
and gone downstairs.

I clambered over the ruptured pavement and through the
wrecked frontage. A carpet of glass and splintered wood lay underfoot. I went down the spiral ornamental iron staircase into a place
I would forever afterwards remember as 'the Pit'.

Daylight filtered in from the hole above, through a dense curtain
woven from a shifting texture of smoke, steam and dust. The light
played weakly on the wreckage of walls and partitions blasted from
the front of the building to the rear. A nauseating, choking stench

filled my nose and lungs: the smell of shattered plasterwork, of burnt explosive, of excrement from the demolished toilets area, of around 500 pounds of mince that had been waiting to be turned into beefburgers. Darkest of all was the distinctive odour of shattered body tissue.

Water had flooded in from the wrecked plumbing and still dripped somewhere in the noisome gloom. I carefully picked my way through the debris into the heart of what was left of the Wimpy Bar. The body was at my feet.

Though on the brief, blurred journey to Oxford Street I had been praying that this was not what I would find, a deeper certainty had refused to be dislodged. In the confusion of radio messages and absence of details, a faint possibility remained that the duty Expo had somehow escaped the blast. No one had known for sure what had happened – no one in the Control Room, no one even here at the scene. I had kept telling myself that there was still a chance, not only because of all the uncertainty but also because I knew this man, the duty Expo. I knew him like a brother, knew how he thought and worked and acted. It seemed inconceivable that a professional of his calibre could have died here.

It lay half-covered with debris. The injuries were massive; death would have occurred instantly.

I glanced away to adjust my eyes to the gloom. White steam eddied wraith-like above and around the wreckage. Sounds registered with painful clarity: the hissing of broken pipes, the bubbling of liquid, the muted creak and crash of debris as it went through another phase of settlement.

I looked at the body again, knowing what it had been, but knowing, too, that at this moment all emotion had to be suspended. An identical device was waiting for me at Debenhams. What had happened here could tell me what I would very soon have to face there.

Body tissue is remarkably resilient; it has to be very close to a bomb if the blast is to destroy it. That was obviously the case here;

even though the body was lying about nine yards from the seat of
the explosion, the type and extent of injury indicated that the
deceased had been looking at the bomb, his face close to it, probably touching something when the explosion occurred. But I
needed to be sure.

Slowly, carefully, I ran my hands down the sides of the body,
sensing rather than seeing its mutilated shape. The action confirmed what I had half-expected: both arms had been blown off by
the explosion. This meant he had been handling or working on the
bomb at the time it went off. It also meant the device probably had
a particularly nasty booby-trap mechanism. The Debenhams bomb
could well be the same.

I stayed alone in the smoking, stinking gloom of that basement
for only a few minutes, for only as long as it took to confirm that
a death had occurred and learn whatever lessons that death could
impart. I did not relate the death to the name or the name to the
man – not while I was checking the body nor when I began a hasty
search of the wreckage, only too well aware that there were only
a few moments in which to seek out a clue to the nature of the
device, some fragment of a component which would tell its own
story. A live bomb was waiting for me.

Then my fingers closed on something soft, something about the
size of my hand. It drew together and crumpled in my grip. At first
I didn't recognize it. I had to look closely, sensing its significance
before understanding its meaning: a piece of cardigan – that old
cardigan Ken always wore. The connections were coming too fast,
were hooking up at a speed that if allowed to go unchecked would
forge link after link after link, each more binding, each more painful, and each more immobilizing than the one before.

I went quickly up the spiral staircase before the connections
could be complete. Every emotion was back in place – apart from
the anger.

It took only a minute to get out of the building, into the Range
Rover and down Oxford Street to Debenhams. Sidestreets and

corners were packed with police and pedestrians, fire engines and ambulances, taxis bumper to bumper behind bright red London Transport double-decker buses. In different circumstances, those moments would have been fuelled by tension and adrenalin. Now something altogether blacker had threaded its way through.

I wanted that bomb. I wanted to get into Debenhams and find the thing and take it apart piece by piece and bit by bit so that we would have every last clue to the identity of those who had made it and planted it, every last microscopic fragment of forensic evidence which would help to nail the bastards who had just killed my best friend.

Tom Brogan, Debenhams' Security Manager, was waiting for me, a lone figure in an eerily empty store. All the lights were on, all the counters stocked and waiting, even the faces of the cash registers glowing.

'Have you been to the one up the road?' Brogan asked me.

I nodded. 'Yes.'

'I've heard a man's been killed . . . ?'

'Yes. But we don't know the circumstances.' I didn't want to talk about it.

He led me through the store, helpfully explaining that the device had been discovered by the Floor Manager who had checked the gents' toilets on the first floor and found three of the cubicle doors closed with the engaged signs showing. He had looked underneath two and seen the occupants' feet; as the third seemed empty he had opened the door and found the packages resting close together on top of the boxed-in cistern: two packages, just like the Wimpy Bar.

After the Security Manager had confirmed the situation, the cubicle door had been closed and the lock turned; there was no exterior handle to open it again so I would have to insert something to turn the lock. I fumbled in my pockets as we walked along, found a 2p piece and stuck it to my hand with adhesive tape – better to do it now than have to fiddle around at the scene.

The occupants of the other cubicles had, predictably, neither seen nor heard anything. As soon as security staff had banged on their doors and told them to leave because of the presence of a suspected bomb, one had emerged from the cubicle like a sprinter off the block, running out into the store and trying to fasten his trousers at the same time. The other, however, had flushed the toilet, emerged properly dressed, closed the door, and gone to the washbasin, where he had insisted on completing his ablutions despite the urgings of the increasingly frantic chaperones. 'Don't you know,' he said, 'it's unhygienic not to wash your hands after using the lavatory?'

In different circumstances I would have probably smiled. At times like this people did the most peculiar things. What concerned me, however, was the disturbance caused by the flushing of toilets and the banging of doors. I didn't know how sensitive the device was but if, for instance, the timer was stuck, then all these separate vibrations could have started it again. The bomb might be running on a one-hour timer, but sixty minutes had long passed since the time of the warning, which meant that it could go off within the next few moments. Even if there was a two-hour delay I didn't have much time to play with.

I parted company with Tom Brogan some twenty yards from the gents' toilets and told him to wait outside the store. I went inside and confronted the locked door. I then discovered I'd parted company with something else: the 2p piece. Somewhere en route it must have dropped from the adhesive tape. I cursed inwardly and went back out into the furnishing department.

The set-piece was a dinner table dressed for eight with crockery and cutlery and all the attendant glassware. It looked very inviting; it also looked strange, like a formal version of the scene aboard the *Marie Celeste*. I grabbed a dinner knife, went back to the cubicle, looked over the top to ensure the door wasn't booby-trapped, and then turned the locking mechanism with the tip of the knife.

The package and the box were less than a yard from me – a main charge and a timer and power unit, linked by wires. I moved closer, feeling an urge to expose their secrets by taking them apart with my hands. But if emotion now stirred after what had happened to Ken, it had to be under complete control.

As I leaned forward to take a closer look, my head touched the partition wall above the device. Amplified by the cavity and the built-in toilet cistern, the tick of a Memo Park timer sounded distinctly in my ears.

I struggled to manoeuvre the X-ray into the confined space. I wanted close, clear shots of both parts of the device, but no matter how I tried, I couldn't achieve an angle which would give me a picture of the base of the main charge. I reluctantly discarded the X-ray and stared hard at the bomb as though by sheer intensity of gaze I could somehow divine within it whatever anti-handler mechanism was waiting for me. Whatever it was that had killed Ken.

The seconds ticked away. Unfortunately there was no chance of getting into the thing by hand. I would have to use the disrupter.

I positioned it in such a way that the high-velocity jet would take out the main charge only. The disrupter was wedged into place with a squishy wet mass of toilet paper which I tore from all the available rolls and then soaked in the lavatory bowl. I ran the firing cable out from the gents' toilets and into the store where I up-ended a settee to create a kind of sentry-box, hid behind it, and then fired. There was a distant *thump!* but no explosion.

I returned to the toilets to discover that the disrupter had been rather too successful: it had shattered both the main charge and the separate timer/power unit. I went down on hands and knees, searching amongst the fragments, more angry now than ever before. The shock and pain of Ken Howorth's death had yet to flood in, had yet to get past the defences that had enabled me to cope with the horror of the Wimpy Bar basement and come straight to this job. Now there was only this deep and burning anger and the furious hope that this debris, this evidence now scattered around me, would one day convict Ken's killers.

Finally I finished with the scene, satisfied myself everything was safe, and left. I handed the dinner knife back to the Security Manager, saying that I had borrowed it for the job. (For a few weeks after the incident the knife was on show in a special glass case bearing the legend: THIS KNIFE WAS USED TO DEFUZE AN IRA BOMB FOUND IN THIS STORE ON OCTOBER 26TH. It wasn't strictly true, but it showed that when you invested in Debenhams' best silverplate, you got far more than you expected at the price.)

The search at Bourne and Hollingsworth had been temporarily suspended in case the alleged bomb was operating on a two-hour timer. The crowds still waited behind the cordons, rank after rank of bobbing white faces, the rooflines of stationary cars and taxis almost hidden in the mêlée. I waited with the search team until the two-hour mark had elapsed, then returned to the Wimpy Bar and went back down into the Pit.

The body was still lying where I had found it; a doctor had arrived but attendance was merely for the record. Officers from the Anti-Terrorist Squad were also there so I briefed them on the scene, then began the clear-up, supervising the work as we painstakingly picked our way through the stinking semi-darkness.

Bourne's was now being searched again, and that meant I needed to be there: the probability was still high that a third bomb was waiting somewhere in the store. So for the rest of that afternoon and evening I alternated between the Wimpy Bar and Bourne's, where sniffer dogs and their handlers worked slowly and methodically through every floor and every item of goods.

I found myself being quietly escorted by the dog-handlers, people who knew how close Ken and I had been and seemed to understand that at this time it would be best if I wasn't left alone. They never said as much, but their expressions and their voices were comforting and I was grateful.

By the time the clock struck midnight I had spent more than
ght hours in perpetual motion between Bourne's and Debenhams
d the Wimpy Bar, also dealing with other suspect devices in the
cinity: three briefcases, eight shopping bags, five packages, one
ck, one pot plant, and one paperweight. All turned out to be
nocuous.

Shortly before the search of Bourne and Hollingsworth was
alled off I was outside on the pavement, having just trudged back
om dealing with yet another suspect device around the corner. It
ad again turned out to be harmless.

Tiredness had not yet hit me, but I knew I needed a moment or
vo to wind down from this latest suspect IED incident before
oing back into Bourne's. A senior Metropolitan Police officer
ddenly appeared – a man almost certainly under as great a strain
s the rest of us and who knew what had happened in Oxford
treet that day. He smiled at me but seemed to have difficulty in
nding something to say. Finally he managed a brisk pleasantry:
You had a busy day, Mr Gurney?'

'Yes.'

'Come on in a hurry, did you?'

'I did, actually.'

'I thought so.' He paused. 'It's normal for you to wear a suit,
n't it?'

Even as he said the words, I suspected he regretted them. Yes,
was true I usually wore a suit. And yes, I wasn't wearing one
ow, there hadn't been time. I was standing outside Bourne and
Hollingsworth in flannel trousers and tie-less shirt and bomber
acket under my flak jacket and I was also covered in blood and
hit and dirt and very probably stinking to high Heaven.

He had been trying to make a joke, I could tell; trying with
umbersome, heavy-handed humour to say something which
eflected the mood and the speed of recent hours. I couldn't believe
hat an officer of that calibre had actually meant what he'd said;
ou would have had to be certifiable to want to conduct a sartorial

inspection at the height of a terrorist outrage. Give him the benef
of the doubt, I told myself.

But then one of the dog-handlers stepped forward and con
fronted a man who was very much his senior in rank. Slowly an
deliberately the dog-handler said: 'D'you want to fucking hit him
Peter, or shall I?'

The moment seemed to freeze: me, the dog-handler, and one c
the Met's top-ranking police officers, the three of us at almo
midnight in a near-deserted Oxford Street, three people at the er
of a day none of us would ever forget.

It could have gone either way. But then the senior officer too
a step back. 'I didn't mean anything,' he said. And it was over. H
footsteps echoed on the pavement; slowly exhaled breath hung c
the night air.

I turned to my companion, my police constable friend. He wou
have done it, I thought, and thrown away his entire career. I didr
say anything but offered up a silent prayer of thanks that the offic
had summed up the situation, realized his gaffe, and been ma
enough to ignore the blatant disrespect of his rank.

Eventually I made it back to the Bungalow and poured myse
a stiff drink. The place was packed; everyone seemed to be c
duty, so I slept on the floor of the Operations Room, still wearin
my flak jacket because I was too tired to take it off.

There had been no time to dwell on anything other than th
events of the moment. I didn't want to think, anyway, because
had already assimilated Ken's death. Even when I glanced at b
desk and saw his coffee mug and his pens, it was all right; I w
reconciled to the way in which little things would sometimes spa
off a memory.

The next day the search resumed at Bourne and Hollingswor
a task the like of which I had never before witnessed. It w
London's largest department store, an unimaginably vast acrea
of floors, and the bomb could be anywhere. The tension never
up, nor the thought that something could happen to someone

ny second. It could be a man on the floor above or below, or the
man next to you. It might be you.

There were thirteen of us, six handlers with their dogs, six police
constables, and myself. It was fortunate none of us were super-
stitious.

From time to time I checked to see how the police constables
were managing. Of course the public never sees this kind of operation and the critics remain unaware of the bravery routinely dis-
played on their behalf. There were young policemen here who had
little thought that morning that an armchair or a sofa would be
viewed with terror. Knowing what might lie hidden, they had to
lift those cushions and probe with trembling fingers. I watched
them, and respected them, and got on with my own search. The
dog-handlers stayed close.

Then, for the second time in twenty-four hours, I had cause to
be grateful to these redoubtable companions. Aware of the need to
ease the pressure and provide some brief distraction, the dog-
handlers took it upon themselves to stage . . . a fashion show.

Dog-handlers are, in the main, built on rather generous lines –
it is unusual for them to be anything less than 6 feet tall and 16
stone. As officers of the Law, they are invaluable; as fashion
models, eccentric. Three of them provided the impromptu display
in the third-floor ladies' lingerie department; dressed in exotic
underwear chosen from the rails and display cases, they paraded
in everything from basques to French knickers (with their dogs in
matching ensembles). Applause and laughter echoed around the
vast empty building; there was something surreal about the scene
and the circumstances. Obviously, such behaviour was against all
regulations but breaking the rules was as nought compared to
breaking the tension.

The search resumed with morale higher than it had ever been,
with spirits lifted and a renewed determination to seek out the
hidden bomb regardless of the threat it posed.

But in the end no bomb was ever found; the store was handed

back to its management. The decision to do so was not taken lightly, but in the absence of evidence there was no other course of action. It seemed that the IRA had pursued a standard terrorist tactic: to strain our resources to the utmost by planting two bombs and then making a hoax call to divert and distract us still further.

Meanwhile a forensic examination was being undertaken of the bomb that had killed Ken and the bomb I had disrupted at Debenhams. The report came through some time later. The Wimpy Bar bomb had indeed incorporated a particular type of anti-handling device. Curiously enough, mine had not.

The funeral service was held in the chapel at Chelsea Barracks. All the Met's explosives officers, past and present, were there. Afterwards, a private service was held at a crematorium not far from Ken's Berkshire home. Like the chapel service, this passed in a kind of blur, very little filtering through except for an awareness of how brave they were in their grief: Anne, Ken's widow, their son Steven, then twenty-one, and daughter Sue, still in her early teens. For myself, I knew that the pain and the sense of loss was too great to invite consideration at that time.

So many memories of my own life were bound up with Ken, with the jobs we had done together, with the places we had visited, with the bad and fun times: the night we frightened them all with the mock Ansaphone message, the day we worked our way through the wreckage of the Iranian Embassy, the evenings the three of us spent at the Bungalow, sipping our whiskies, Roger making his point and Ken saluting back.

But Roger was gone, and now Ken. I knew the names of other friends would come too – friends who, it had seemed, would always be around at the end of the day. But they were gone, and only memories remained; like Alan Brahmer that day on our parachute training when he hauled himself back up to talk about Geronimo. Alan, killed in Northern Ireland.

I knew instinctively that the floodgates must not be allowed to open then, in the aftermath of Ken's death. Ken Howorth hadn't died just so his best friend could fall apart. The living have an obligation to the dead as well as to themselves. So I worked on, blocking out yesterday, dealing only with today, as I had done that day at the Wimpy Bar.

It was only that piece of cardigan, a ragged patch of wool, torn and shredded and singed by the fireball, which got through my defences.

In midsummer 1983 I learned that, in recognition of our work in October 1981, Ken had been posthumously awarded a George Medal and I had been awarded a Bar to go with the George Medal I'd already won in Northern Ireland.

The presentation was made by the Queen at Buckingham Palace. For a very long time, it seemed, she talked to me, remembering my previous George Medal and MBE for gallantry. We discussed the events and the jobs I had dealt with in London, and then she said that, earlier that day, she had had a private investiture of the George Medal to Mr Howorth's widow. 'Did you know him at all?' she asked.

Surprised, I said, 'Of course I knew him. He was my closest friend for twenty-five years, Ma'am.'

'But you went in and examined the body –' The Queen stopped in mid-sentence, as if picturing the scene in her mind. There was no mistaking the sorrow on her face as the silence seemed to run on endlessly between us.

After she had hooked my little Bar with its small piece of ribbon to my chest, I went out into a Palace anteroom to collect the box. I knew Honours boxes could be very impressive; I couldn't wait to see what they had come up with this time – Moroccan red leather, or maybe tiny quilts of velvet. A gentleman in a morning suit consulted his list while I stared at the table between us. It was stacked with boxes, all of them as dignified as that which they were intended to accommodate.

'Mr Gurney?' said the man with the boxes. 'Bar to the George

Medal?' He rummaged around under the table and handed me a very small self-seal plastic bag.

I stared from him to the bag and back again. 'There isn't a box?'

'No,' he said cheerfully. 'That's it.'

That night at Cannon Row Police Station the Expos staged a celebration party. The centrepiece of the room was a table on which they had placed a velvet cushion with my Bar resting in the middle and an enormous desktop magnifying glass, used for forensic examination, set above that.

Also on the cushion was the resealable plastic bag and a note saying: PLEASE RETURN TO BUCKINGHAM PALACE AFTER USE. I still have happy memories of the night. And, naturally, I still have the plastic bag.

I also remember thinking at the time how much Ken would have enjoyed it all.

By 1984 it was becoming increasingly obvious that, like any other organization, the Metropolitan Police Explosives Office needed a formal structure. Until then, all explosives officers were considered equal; being the type of people they were, Expos were not concerned with conventional preoccupations like rank or status or promotion because when you're out on the street facing the challenge of a bomb your performance is measured by rather different criteria than apply elsewhere.

Even so, some form of leadership seemed desirable. Though we managed the functions of the office in such a way that duties were shared out amongst ourselves – for instance, one Expo would be responsible for admin, another for ongoing training, another for looking after the secret library – the vagaries of the shift system meant you could go for long periods without ever seeing a particular colleague.

A point, a person, to whom all Expos could go and all outsiders contact made sense. But who? When the idea was first mooted by the Met, it was suggested that someone be brought in to head up

e office. In a rare gesture of unanimity (it was one of the few
:casions when all Expos agreed with each other) the notion was
jected: we took the view that not only were we the most com-
etent and experienced at this kind of EOD work, we didn't feel
ny outsider would be technically qualified or know enough about
ir working methods and conditions to run the team.

And so the ball was bounced back into our court: who, we were
ked, do you think should do the job? The answer was a collective
b of the thumb in my direction: 'him'.

Thus it was that on 21 October 1985 I became head of the
letropolitan Police Explosives Office. I was pleased, not a little
attered, and delighted not so much that I'd been given the job as
ven the trust of friends and colleagues. The most important thing
f all was that this collection of pretty unique individuals were
omfortable with the thought that yes, they could rely on me, that
knew what the job was like, the problems, the frustrations, the
allenges. That I knew and understood their fears in a way no
utsider ever could.

It did not of course mean that the working atmosphere suddenly
anged: logically, the head of an office is the chief officer, but a
tle of that nature didn't fit the group's sense of humour. Chief
xplosives Officer was not a term to conjure with, whereas Senior
xplosives Officer ... that was *much* better. SEXPO.

But the way I viewed the Sexpo's role was not the way the Met
iewed it; early on the assumption was made that this new, senior
ost would be non-operational, that the Sexpo would undertake a
orking day much like any other manager. I violently disagreed:
was my belief that no one could head an operation such as this
ithout active participation in its work. You had to know what it
as like, out there on the streets, you had to stay in touch with
e changing trends and innovations in terrorism at first-hand, not
ia the experiences of others or neatly stacked pages of official
ports. A good boss should always be interested in the work of
is team and the challenges they face but there's nothing like

risking your own life as an incentive to keeping up to date wit
what's happening all around.

The early days, then, were difficult: although the Sexpo jo
description didn't require me to work shifts, we were so unde
staffed that it would have been impractical, not to say irresponsib
of me, to stick to the letter of my contract. I therefore found myse
working very long hours; the conventional hours of a manager a
well as doing operational shifts around the clock.

I might have been earning a higher salary, but the gap betwee
theory and practice was wide: for instance, I no longer qualifie
for either extra payment or time off in lieu of weekend workin
the thought rapidly dawned that if I'd been blown up by a bon
on a Sunday afternoon then insult would have compounded fat
injury – I'd have departed this life in my own time and at my ow
expense . . .

Fortunately, as soon as the Met discovered what was happenin
steps were immediately taken to deal with the problem. The resu
meant that I could go on being both Expo and Sexpo and be pa
for the privilege.

It all meant I could go on being The Bomb Burglar.

The nickname came about as much as a result of circumstan
as my own enthusiasm for the work. Every bomb situation
frightening. But every bomb situation is *interesting* – you simp
don't know what you'll find.

All Expos are fascinated by bombs otherwise they wouldn't
the job. Cliché or not, EOD is a way of life: the challenge of t
unknown is a constancy. The next bomb could well be of a desi
and type you've encountered before, but it could also be somethi
entirely new, something which will test your skills and judgeme
to the full.

Which meant I couldn't just sit behind my desk when a call ca
in, knowing that a situation would have to wait because the du
Expos were all out on jobs. I had to get my things together a
go. Duty calls, I'd tell myself, but the other Expos tended to rega

h behaviour with a wry smile. Said one of them: 'I've only got
be in the loo when the Hotline rings and by the time I've come
, Peter's already half-way to the job.'

In a different kind of job, in a different type of organization, this
t of behaviour could well have been counter-productive. The
plosives Office, though, is different; what welds its members
ether is a spirit and self-motivation of a very unique kind.

So yes, some of my colleagues might've grumbled about The
mb Burglar. But they also knew that as long as Gurney was
king bombs rather than counting paper clips, the danger of the
ganization becoming just another component of a bureaucratic
chine was very remote indeed.

12

Still Here

===

17 December 1983: the Saturday before Christmas. I was drivi
home when I heard the news on my car radio. There had beer
bomb explosion outside Harrods. I stopped the car and used
payphone to tell the office I was coming back in. Then I rang
driver and asked him if he'd come back too.

By the time I arrived at the Bungalow there were a number
jobs waiting to be dealt with. The Expo on the scene at Harr
was apparently going to be there for quite a while. I cleared
other jobs and then, when things slackened off, went over
Knightsbridge. Three hours had elapsed since the blast. I thoug
my colleague might appreciate assistance or a break.

There was the usual chaos in the vicinity of the incident, peo
milling about and traffic jammed up in all directions because of
closure of the main thoroughfare. I found my colleague gather
debris for forensic analysis and asked his permission to enter
area (an Expo never sets foot on another's patch without conse

It was quiet around Harrods. Quiet and still and empty exc
for a couple of police officers. In the glare of the streetlamp
found myself walking across ice – no, not ice: though the wh
area was glistening as if dressed for the season it was actua

ered with glass, with shards and fragments of what had once
n the store windows. In some places the glass was ankle deep.
runched underfoot or shifted under the weight of my passing
falls, tinkling. .

he bomb had been placed in an old car parked facing the wrong
r in a narrow one-way street alongside Harrods. A warning had
n given by the IRA but the wording was deliberately ambiguous.
e police were evacuating the scene when the bomb exploded.

looked at the dimly lit and shattered showcase displays, now
n to the night air and a wind which chafed at ragged Christmas
orations, which stirred at torn drapes and made them slowly
ow. In buildings higher up the street, fairy lights continued to
h. Everywhere I looked I could see evidence of the season of
dwill to all men – wrapping paper, presents in pretty boxes,
bles, decorations, twisted strands of Christmas Tree lights.

. . *jingle all the day, oh what fun it is to ride in a one-horse open
gh . . . Oh . . . Jingle bells, jingle bells, jingle all the way . . .*'
he sound suddenly surged and ebbed. Then came: *I'm dreamin'
e White Christmas . . . Just like the Christmas cards I write . . .*' The
oes were now gilded with a sweet sentimentality.

he strangely scented air was now overpowering, drenching the
ht with sweetness. The blast had swept through the store's
metics and perfumery counters. Now, though, different scents
ailed me: burnt oil, burnt rubber, the smell of explosive, the
nch of burnt flesh.

Beneath the car lay the body of a police officer. He had been
ing to get people to safety when the bomb went off and blew
vehicle into the air. It had come down on top of him. In the
ce fire that followed, both car and victim had been consumed.
w there was only a tangled mass of burnt metal, an unidentifi-
e body beneath it. From underneath the remains of the car a
d pointed straight up into the air as if reaching out for help.

Near by, another victim lay in the sparkling debris. He was very
, maybe 6 feet 4 inches, with only one apparent injury, the result

of a fragment striking him in the middle of his forehead. If he'
not been so tall, the splinter would have missed and he'd still hav
been alive.

I moved away, still conscious of the Christmas music, still fight
ing the nausea of the Christmas smell and the other darker scent
behind.

The third body was a young woman. She had been blow
through a plate-glass window and lay tumbled and broken upo
the tide of gaily coloured wreckage. At first I thought she was
mannequin. Her skirt had been blown off and she was wearing
little pair of panties decorated with a heart which embraced th
message: I LOVE YOU.

The safety switch on which I had so long depended failed me
that moment.

Who had she been, this girl? For whom had she worn the
clothes? Who had she loved, and who had loved her? I LOVE YO

Too late I became aware of what was happening: I was breaki
the unwritten rules which said I should remain detached. The bo
of a victim is a clue – sometimes, a vital clue – to the nature a
performance of a bomb. To consider the victim as a person is
make a bad situation far worse. Bomb scenes are frightening pla
to be and a confident, controlled and detached explosives officer
essential to the whole operation. If an Expo is upset, is in te
or racked by anger, then that will show. If he is frightened, t
will show too. If he lets anything in from outside it will disr
him deep within, and when that happens everything can co
apart.

I turned away and headed back to the cordon and the metrono
sweep of dozens of blue lights. I had gone to Harrods as one w
has a professional interest in bombs, but because I had no act
role to play I had nothing to stop my mind from ranging into ar
filled only with a sense of painful futility.

Later, in the safety of home, the tears finally came.

*

The capability of the IRA to wreak havoc and terror on the mainland population shows little sign of diminishing. In the early 1970s, IRA strategists circulated an internal document which showed how economic damage running into millions could be caused by incendiary devices costing only a few pounds. Twenty years on, that strategy still holds true: IRA incendiary attacks continue to demonstrate the scale of disruption and destruction which can be inflicted at minimal expense to the perpetrators.

In many ways this is a textbook example of what happens when society inadvertently allows itself to be terrorized, for the threat posed by this kind of campaign is magnified out of all proportion thanks to over-reaction by the authorities and over-emphasis by the media. Such ill-judged behaviour is not lost on the IRA; it now knows that even a series of hoax calls, interspersed with the odd incendiary or two, can paralyse large areas of London and other major UK towns and cities.

The future is therefore likely to see a continuation of the existing pattern of tactics: shootings, hoaxes, bombs of increasing technological sophistication and what might best be termed as 'pot-boilers' and 'spectaculars', the former covering incendiary attacks and small explosive devices, the latter major attacks such as those at the Baltic Exchange in the City, and Staples Corner, where a vital artery in London's road system was all but destroyed.

The importance of the 'pot-boiler' (as well as the hoax) derives as much from what it is as what it represents: a further drain on security and police resources and a niggling reminder to society at large that the IRA is by no means a spent force. By contrast, the 'spectaculars' exist not only to cause widespread damage but to keep the terrorists on the front page, to demonstrate that at any time the IRA is capable of major attacks.

Paradoxically, official response to both types of incident has been consistently inappropriate: the 'pot-boiler' has been played up, but the 'spectacular' played down, resulting in widespread misreporting. Although the media was told that both the City and Staples

Corner devices were of the order of 100 pounds of Semtex, even from my cursory examinations of the bomb scenes the devastation shows the magnitude to have been far in excess of that – I estimate between 750 and 1,000 pounds of home-made explosive.

I am at a loss to explain why the facts were not properly disclosed; as the IRA know the size of the devices they used, there is little point in withholding the information from everyone else. A further consideration also arises: anyone seeing the pictures of the aftermath of Staples Corner and the Baltic Exchange could be forgiven for thinking that if the terrorists can do so much damage with just 100 pounds of explosive, what could they do with a much *bigger* bomb?

The fiction which began with Semtex – that the IRA was somehow in possession of a 'super-weapon' – thus runs on unchecked as the terrorists are handed another undeserved propaganda victory. The lesson is simple: whenever the facts are needlessly obscured or withheld, it is to the terrorist's benefit, not society's.

The Harrods' bombing was the one occasion when my internal safety switch failed to work. On the whole I have managed to maintain the detached attitude so crucial to the work of bomb disposal. And our professionalism is constantly being put to the test: Andy Clarke, the Explosives Officer I worked with during the London car bomb campaign of March 1973, once found himself on the receiving end of a ferocious cross-examination by a defence counsel.

The Court case had nothing to do with terrorism – the accused was actually charged with safe-blowing. Andy, who had been tasked to the scene, made notes of what he had found there and what he had done and then wrote what should have been a comprehensive report. Unfortunately Andy was better at practice than theory; give him an incident to deal with and he would manage just fine, but give him a sheet of paper and a typewriter and he stared at the page in frustration.

I knew how he felt. All my life I've hated paperwork too. Unfor

..nately this kind of antipathy can cause problems, especially when
. leaves you open to challenge as an expert witness. You know
vhat you did and why you did it, but if you haven't explained
verything in writing, then others can attack your professional
redibility.

The defence counsel tore into Andy. 'So you're saying you *did*
..arry out this particular procedure at the scene?'

'Yes, sir.'

'But it isn't mentioned in your report.'

'No, sir.'

'Just like this other business, about what happened with the safe.
That isn't fully explained in your report, either.'

'No, sir.'

Counsel turned theatrically to the Court, then back to Andy
..gain. 'You're not a very good explosives officer are you, Mr
Clarke?'

'Well,' said Andy, 'I'm still here ...'

Still here: two words that separate the lucky from the unlucky.
From those who make one mistake too many and those who do
..ot. Still here, after all the years of tension and fear and close
.ncounters with death. If you've gone into high-risk situations time
..nd again and survived them, then you're a very good explosives
.fficer indeed.

But the day comes when you can't do it any longer. The pressure
.ecomes too great, or ill-health intervenes, or you come up against
he one obstacle that can't be surmounted: retirement age. Retire-
.ent at sixty is compulsory. To an Expo whose nature is not to
.hink that far ahead, retirement age is something that belongs to
.nother day and comes to other people.

When it came to me, I could have done without it. Someone
.aid it was quite a distinction, reaching retirement age while still
.n 'active service'; someone else said, Aren't you glad, no more of
his charging about London, never knowing from one day to the
.ext what will happen?

I didn't reply. I didn't know if I was supposed to feel or look any different. I was the same person who not long before had been sitting astride a mortar at the back of 10 Downing Street: same person, same year, but different age.

It seemed to take for ever, parcelling up my things, emptying my office, taking home all the unlikely little souvenirs that had accumulated over the years. It also seemed as much like the beginning as the ending, for the view beyond the window showed a scene little changed from the day I first joined the Met's Explosives Office: the capital still spread out beneath a grey winter sky; the Thames still flowed sluggishly under Westminster Bridge.

Later there were parties, many of them connected with the Met, several of them not, social gatherings or festivities prompted by the Christmas season or the dawn of 1992. They were all in their separate ways enjoyable, but the best were the family parties, because no questions were asked, so no answers had to be given.

My son and daughter were grown up now, with careers of their own. As for Daphne and me, we had long since parted. Our marriage had slowly run down to the point where there had been little sense in staying together. I left with no thought of marrying again, but then in the spring of 1983 I met Sheridan, a journalist; we were married seven years later.

Sheridan was, and is, very special. For the first time ever I found myself truly sharing my work and my experiences with someone who listened and understood. She brought with her a new perspective, a new way of looking at the world; she raised questions and issues which made me re-evaluate many of the things I had previously found it easier to shelve. I realized then that I had been carrying too many pieces of locked baggage filled with suppressed memories.

Although it was never easy to field a ready answer, I began to find it less awkward to respond to the questions that people always asked about a way of life that seemed quite inexplicable. The answers were not always what people expected; it is human nature to prefer intrigue to clarity, complexity to simplicity. Yet the answer to the recurring question was always simple: I did what I did because I enjoyed it and it challenged me. How others in bomb disposal felt about their jobs I couldn't say, although it was obvious that what bound us together transcended routine considerations like salaries and working conditions. I could only speak for myself, and say that I'd had a lifetime of bombs because I had never wanted anything else.

There was one other question, asked sometimes directly, sometimes obliquely, that always touched upon the soul of the bomb man's existence: how it is that he can continue day after day, knowing the risks.

Bomb disposal operators may discuss each other's ideas, problems, past mistakes and even near-disasters – the times when we've all thought, Oh Christ! this is the end of the line – but they don't debate their innermost feelings. They don't bring to the surface their fears and anxieties because to do so is to tread on dangerous ground; to do so is to bring to light something an individual might not wish (or be strong enough) to confront.

Over the years, in various parts of the world, I've seen what happens as a result. I've seen men exhaust their last reserve of courage and, instead of acknowledging it and realizing that there's no shame, no dishonour in losing the nerve to go on, have thrown themselves into ever more dangerous situations, taking risks that beggared belief.

To their way of thinking, they've been testing themselves to the full, braving everything and defying anything which might compel them to give up their career. But an operator who is unable to maintain mastery over fear is an operator who shouldn't be there; the risk posed by a bomb going off is already great and an operator who is coming apart is only adding to that risk.

Bomb disposal men are conscious of the strength of nerve that is required, but it isn't at the forefront of their minds. To the

bomb man, bravery isn't some swaggering display, some gung-ho
exhibition of macho bravado. It is the mastery of fear, a mastery
often maintained by sheer strength of will, which provides the
adrenalin vital to take one through a testing situation. Above all,
it is knowledge that sustains daily existence: the years of training,
the accumulation of experience. It is knowledge that shores up
a sometimes faltering heart, and underpins a faith in one's own
professionalism, a belief in one's own abilities to tackle whatever
the day may bring.

As the years go by, that knowledge grows, and though deep
down the fear never fades, the degree of fear changes according to
circumstance and experience, until the time comes when, if you're
frightened, you are very, very frightened because you *know* you
have every reason to be.

I never felt fear when I was young; in a sense, it had to be
acquired, like experience, over the years. When you're young you
think you're immortal; later though, in Belfast and London, I realized I was wrong.

Understanding did not come overnight; it emerged from the slow
erosion of youthful certainties. It came little by little with every
job and, particularly, it came with the hours spent between tasks,
when fear can suddenly begin to throb, when it can threaten to
burst forth and drown you in a freezing terror. That's when you
have to remind yourself of all the things you've learned, the things
you've achieved. That's when you have to exert mastery over fear
by reassuring yourself that yes, you know enough to go out there
and deal with the unknown.

To outsiders, of course, it's all inexplicable, because there is no
commonality of experience, no shared understanding of what the
bomb man's work entails. People sometimes ask me: 'How many
real bombs have you done, then?' and I've said, 'A few hundred'
and they've said, 'Oh', as if disappointed. They don't know about
the thousands of false alarms, hoaxes and suspect devices which
have had to be dealt with; the boxes and the parcels which only

proved innocent *after* they'd tested every last resource, mental as well as physical.

So the answer to the question is yes, I've been afraid. I've been afraid because a bomb is a deadly thing. If you're not frightened of it then you won't respect it and if you don't respect it then you don't get to live very long. It's a fear that has to be mastered every time you begin the long walk towards something which might explode. You say to yourself, At this point it could injure me ... at this point it might kill me ... and at this point it doesn't matter what I think or hope because now I'm as close as I'll ever be, and if I've arrived at the precise moment when a timer initiates detonation ...

Luck, skill, knowledge, experience, fear, and strength of will – you need all of them in their correct proportion, and if the day comes when you're convinced they're out of balance, that your luck is running out or your knowledge is inadequate or the fear has grown too strong to be mastered, then that is the day you should stop and say, That's enough.

There's no shame in ending a career by acknowledging that you cannot go on. All human beings are different, and no two bomb men are ever the same.

It's hard, very, very hard, but I've seen it happen to others, and I've understood why. It hasn't diminished them as people and in some ways it has actually enriched them because it takes true courage to face reality and acknowledge that you can no longer contemplate the long walk to the loneliest place in the world.

Only the foolhardy persist in continuing. Braver men walk away.

Epilogue

═══

And so it continues: the bombing of New York's World Trade Center, the devastation of the City of London, the slaughter of children in a northern English town ... Despite the revulsion felt by all decent men and women and the efforts of law enforcement agencies world-wide, international terrorism still practises its lethal trade.

In Britain, the IRA's tactical mix of 'potboilers', 'spectaculars' and hoaxes has made for headlines on a scale not seen since the mid eighties, for whether a small device (the potboiler, so called because it keeps the threat bubbling away in the public's mind) or a large explosion, the impact has been considerable.

The killing of two youngsters in the crowded town centre of War-rington, Cheshire (the charge was probably no more than 1 pound) earned the IRA international condemnation; it also triggered a renewed peace effort on both sides of the Irish border. But only time will tell if the latest outburst of popular opinion has any more effect today than it did in the mid 1970s. Even the fact that the IRA *appeared* to switch tactics after Warrington – from soft civilian targets to high-profile attacks designed to cause commercial chaos – cannot be taken as evidence of a change of heart, for to assume that any terrorist group has a 'heart' smacks of a dangerous naivety.

I doubt very much if the IRA will, as some have suggested, 'learn a lesson' from Warrington. After all, no long-term change occurred in the wake of the Harrods attack or the Enniskillen Remembrance Day slaughter: the bombers simply waited until the fuss died down and then went back to killing as and when it suited. Warrington might be 1993's byword for the depths to which the IRA will stoop, but there's no guarantee that the name of another town or city won't take its place in the future.

In terrorist terms, Warrington succeeded (because it terrorized). In propaganda terms, however, the City of London attack probably achieved far more, demonstrating as it did the IRA's capacity to deal a major blow to the nerve centre of the UK's financial community. Results also lived up to the IRA's notion of 'economic warfare', for the reputed £350 million and £500 million it cost to clear up after the Baltic Exchange and Bishopsgate bombs respectively might be seen by the average citizen as money which could well have gone into building new hospitals or schools. And when people think that millions are being 'lost' because of terrorism, public frustration grows ever more acute – precisely as the terrorists intended. Spectacular bombings touch everyone, because ultimately it's the ordinary house-holder who has to foot the bill by way of increased insurance premiums, or higher taxation.

The Bishopsgate bomb, housed in a large tipper truck, serves to highlight some of the many difficulties facing a bomb-disposal man, for in such a situation he must (a) try to estimate the possible size of the device so that he can calculate the potentially enormous evacuation area required; (b) legislate for other blast effects which may not be immediately obvious (ruptured gas mains, for instance, and even – in this instance – damage to the London Underground); (c) contend with the almost Herculean task of locating the bomb's fuzing system (about the size of two cigarette packets, and likely to be hidden anywhere).

He must also bear in mind that there may be more than one fuzing system – and booby traps, too. Which means that even if he manages to get into the cab of the suspect vehicle and find a fuzing system and deal with it, he certainly can't rule out the possibility of a second system elsewhere in the vehicle, discovery of which will only be possible by dint of removing the entire contents of the truck, anything up to four *tons* of explosive. (Nevertheless, it is not impossible to defuze very large bombs such as these, as has been shown in the past.)

Prevention is, as ever, better than cure, which explains why, in response to these IRA spectaculars, mainland Britain seems ready to follow the Northern Ireland example by committing a heavy security presence to the streets. To stop the large van and truck bombs, police have initiated stop and search procedures, and even placed armed roadblocks on some of London's and Manchester's thoroughfares. But although such measures are undoubtedly effective, they're extremely costly in terms of police resources, as well as a new and intrusive addition to our day-to-day existence. Unfortunately, though of necessity, they are forced to play the game the terrorists' way, for the IRA's campaign is as much designed to hit the public purse as disrupt the workings of a democratic society.

Where potboilers are concerned, terrorism in its most literal sense is the objective. From a bomb-disposal man's point of view, such a small device is seldom difficult to defuze – it's *finding* them that is the greatest problem. Often, nothing more than a vague, general warning is given (for example, a bomb is in such-and-such a shopping precinct). Warnings are also deliberately issued late, in the hope that the bomb won't be found whilst simultaneously ensuring that the IRA can still stake spurious claim to some kind of moral ground by saying, after the ambulances have departed, well, we were decent enough to tell you.

There is a third kind of tactic in the IRA's strategy: proxy bombing, where the driver of a vehicle is forced to deliver a bomb to a specified target. Fortunately, this tactic is likely to remain unusual in mainland Britain, even though the practice has been followed in Northern Ireland for many years. That it is more prevalent in the latter than the former is due to the comparative strength of the IRA: in Northern Ireland, terrorists have the resources to hold hostage the family of a hijacked person because IRA collaborators and sympathizers exist in far greater number than on the British mainland.

Outrage follows outrage ... and as we approach the millennium there must be many who wonder what kind of world we're now living in. In Britain the thought occurs in the wake of every terrorist attack, its despair given voice by yet another grieving mother, yet another heartbroken husband or wife. What terrorism truly is, and what terrorism truly does, is fully comprehended by a nation which for over twenty years has been sickened by the men (and women) of violence.

By contrast, many a similarly law-abiding citizen of the USA has remained remote from the bomber's threat – indeed, plenty of evidence exists to suggest that some have freely contributed to the terrorist cause, have so misunderstood the evil of the IRA that their dollars have, well-nigh literally, fuelled the flames.

But then came the explosion at the World Trade Center. In a sense it paralleled the City of London attacks, although in New York the much smaller bomb was actually placed inside the building rather than out on the street. It caused considerably more structural damage than if it had exploded outdoors; that the building so well withstood the huge blast says much for the basic strength of its construction.

In another sense though, the New York attack represents far more than a mere echo of that for so long experienced on the other side of the Atlantic. For in demonstrating that terrorism can indeed strike at the heart of *any* community, in *any* civilized society and at *any* time, the World Trade Center bombing will hopefully have driven home the message that as long as terrorism is allowed to flourish, whether by tacit consent or active support, then *everyone* in this global village of ours – children and adults alike – is at risk.

Wider awareness is for the ultimate good of all, for only with a common understanding and a shared determination can society ensure that one door after another is closed to the killers in our midst, leaving them with nowhere to hide, and nowhere to run.

Glossary

═══

AE	Ammunition Examiner (later changed to AT)
AT	Ammunition Technician
ATO	Ammunition Technical Officer
BAD	Base Ammunition Depot
BAOR	British Army of the Rhine
BEA	British European Airways
a 'Blind'	A projectile filled with high explosive, smoke or illuminating composition which has failed to function on impact or arrival at its target
BOAC	British Overseas Airways Corporation
C4	An American-manufactured military plastic explosive
CAD	Central Ammunition Depot
CMD	Conventional Munition Disposal
Co-Op	A 'home-made' high explosive
Cordite	A type of propellant for guns, rockets etc.
Cordtex	The proprietary name for a type of detonating cord
CSM	Company Sergeant Major
CRAOC	Commander Royal Army Ordnance Corps

Detonating cord	A flexible cord containing high explosive which is used to transmit a detonating wave. The cord cannot be ignited, it must be set off by detonation
Detonator	A small device used to initiate detonation
Disrupter	A piece of equipment which fires a jet of water at high speed to 'disrupt' an IED
EOD	Explosive Ordnance Disposal (a generic term covering both CMD and IEDD)
Expo	Explosives Officer
Frangex	A commercial nitroglycerine-based high explosive
Fuze	A mechanical, chemical or electrical mechanism which starts the firing process of an explosive charge
Gelamex	A commercial nitroglycerine-based high explosive
HE	High explosive
IED (D)	Improvized Explosive Device (Disposal)
Incendiary	A bomb designed to cause a fire
IRA	Irish Republican Army
Mercury-tilt switch	A type of electrical switch containing mercury. When the switch is moved, the mercury completes the circuit and triggers an IED
Microswitch	A small electrical switch which is extremely sensitive to pressure
MO	Medical Officer
Mortar	A short-barrelled weapon which is used to launch low-velocity projectiles at high angles
Mortar bomb	A bomb fired from a mortar
MVEE	Military Vehicles Experimental Establishment
NAAFI	Navy, Army, Air Force Institute
NCO	Non-commissioned officer
NG	Nitroglycerine

PE4	A British military plastic explosive
PETN	A commercial and military high explosive
RAOC	Royal Army Ordnance Corps
RDX	A commercial and military high explosive
RE	Royal Engineers
RSM	Regimental Sergeant Major
RUC	Royal Ulster Constabulary
Safety fuse	A cord containing gunpowder which is used to transmit a flame. It can be ignited by a naked flame
Semtex	A plastic explosive manufactured in Czechoslovakia
Sexpo	Senior Explosives Officer
Sten gun	A World War II sub-machine gun
Thyrister	An electronic component
TNT	A high explosive
WO 1	Warrant Officer Class 1
WO 2	Warrant Officer Class 2
WRVS	Women's Royal Voluntary Service

Picture Credits

Index

INDEX